24 HOUR PARTY PEOPLE

The Film Consortium and United Artists present

In association with the Film Council and FilmFour

A Revolution Films production in association with Baby Cow

A Michael Winterbottom Film • Steve Coogan

24 HOUR PARTY PEOPLE

Paddy Considine • Lennie James • John Simm

Casting Wendy Brazington • Costume Designers Natalie
Ward & Stephen Noble • Executive Producer Henry
Normal • Line Producer Robert How • Co-producer
Gina Carter • Director of Photography Robby Müller •
Editor Trevor Waite • Production Designer Mark Tildesley

Screenplay by Frank Cottrell Boyce
Produced by Andrew Eaton
Directed by Michael Winterbottom

TheFilmConsortium   REVOLUTION   PATHÉ!   FILM|COUNCIL

24 HOUR PARTY PEOPLE

What the Sleeve Notes Never Tell You

Anthony Wilson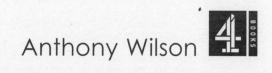

For Izzy and Olly and Vette.

First published in March 2002 by Channel 4 Books, an imprint of Pan Macmillan Ltd,
20 New Wharf Road, London N1 9RR, Basingstoke and Oxford.

Associated companies throughout the world.

www.panmacmillan.com

ISBN 978-0-7522-2025-3

13 15 17 19 18 16 14

A CIP catalogue record for this book is available from the British Library.

Designed and typeset by seagulls
Printed and bound in the UK by CPI Mackays, Chatham ME5 8TD

'Atmosphere' written by Ian Curtis, Peter Hook, Stephen Morris, Bernard Sumner.
Published by Fractured Music (administered by Zomba Music Publishers Ltd).

'Wrote for Luck', 'Tart Tart', 'Kinky Afro' words and music by Shaun Ryder, Paul Ryder,
Mark Day, Paul Davis and Gary Whelan © 2000 London Music, London W6 8BS.
Reproduced by permission of International Music Publications Ltd. All Rights Reserved.

Author photograph by Jon Super © A.H. Wilson.

Photo credits:
THE TRUTH p1 A.H. Wilson; p2 (top) Granada Television, (below) Peter Saville for Factory;
p3 (below left) Jean-Francois Octave for Factory Benelux, (below right) James Martin for Factory;
p4 Kevin Cummins/Idols; p5 (top) Peter Saville for Factory, (below) Chris Taylor/Retna; p6 Peter Saville
for Factory; p7 (top) Derek Ridgers/London Features International Ltd, (below) Vini Reilly for Factory;
p8 (top) A.H. Wilson, (centre) Peter Walsh, (below left) A.H. Wilson, (below right) Simon King.

THE FICTION p9-16 Jon Shard © Film Consortium/Pathe UK 2001; except p9 (top left), p12 (top),
p14 (top), p16 (below) © Amelia Troubridge/Film Consortium/Pathe UK 2001.

The publishers have made every effort to trace the owners
of these photographs, and apologise for any omissions.

Visit **www.panmacmillan.com** to read more about all our books and to buy
them. You will also find features, author interviews and news of any author
events, and you can sign up for e-newsletters so that you're always first to hear
about our new releases.

FOREWORD: 'WHAT'S PAST IS PROLOGUE'

I don't really want to write this foreword.

Never explain.

But thanking people and apologising to people is good form, and we can be formal at this point.

Apparently, I need to explain that this is a novelisation, the turning of a fine movie screenplay into a book. Apparently, novelisation is the lowest form of art which is right up my street.

Being a novelisation means that (a) a lot of what follows is pure bloody fiction and never actually happened and (b) the little genius who made up the series of lies and filth contained in the *24 Hour Party People* movie script is responsible for all the good lines, good jokes and good dialogue that follows hereafter.

This gentleman is a good Catholic boy from Liverpool called Frank Cottrell Boyce. I apologise for mangling his work, and while I'm about it, I apologise for any offence I might cause his home town by the Mersey.

Some people I know think I have a down on Liverpool, and this novelisation may be deemed to contain items of disrespect in that area. Bollocks. Liverpool is Manchester's big brother down the road, our other self, indeed. I will, in the manner of a poor man's Voltaire, defend to the death the right of a man to take the piss out of the next lot down the motorway.

It's a great, great city, but should develop it's sense of humour, perhaps... Time for the 'Thanks' bit, just like the bloody Oscars. When's someone going to say 'Big up' on the big night?

Big up our own movie people, Michael Winterbottom, Andrew Eaton and Frank for wanting to do this story, and getting the feel of the punk gigs and the Hac dance floor exact and perfect. Thanks and congratulations to them and all the Revolution Films people.

Thanks to the fine actors in the movie, several of whom (and especially Steve Coogan), in their ad libbing and development of the script, again provided some of the best bits of this novelisation.

And no, Steve, you're not going to hit me for the royalties.

Thanks to my editor whose patience etc etc etc... Authors always write that stuff. I'm not an author. But Gillian Christie is fucking ace, and all the others at Macmillan. I even let Gillian take out a bit about Manchester being responsible for 11 September, 'cause a Manchester scientist was instrumental in the Balfour declaration. It's the kind of 'true' bullshit I like to write and I let her cut it which shows how much I think of her.

'Il miglior fabbro.' No, it's not better at Faber, it's better at Macmillan.

Think highly of and thank highly Mia Bays of the Film Consortium, who persuaded me into doing this thing and sorted the deal.

And think highly of Ra Page, literary backbone of Manchester's *City Life* magazine, who two years ago hassled me into writing a short story and without whom I would never have set out on this fiction stuff. I'm really a piece-to-camera man, six sentences, well turned and in *Daily Mirror* speak. Thank you Ra for hustling me into semi-art.

Do I thank the characters in this book? The quick and the dead. No. I just need to love 'em. Dead or alive.

Thanks to Mark Twain, whose analysis of truth – that it is our most valauble commodity and therefore should be economised – forms the moral backbone of what is to follow.

And finally, thanks to my partner Yvette for putting up with this *24 Hour Party People* stuff, which involves the baggage that the elder partner always brings to a relationship. And thanks for the wondrous relationship – but that's the next book.

This is this one.

PROLOGUE:
THE WHEEL

Fuck this for a lark.

I am not a quiz show host, nor was ever meant to be.

Friday evening, Studio 2 and the misplaced sentiment was too late. Again.

The opening titles were twenty seconds in and we were already bearing down on the dread moment; that deep, meaningful and totally meaningless voice-over man's powerful invocation:

'Ladies and gentlemen, welcome to *Wheel of Fortune*.'

Wilson takes his cue on the first syllable of 'welcome'. Down the arc of TV-beige carpeted stairs accompanied by the regulation female assistant. They hadn't invented the Vorderman yet, so he had to make do with – God, what was her fucking name?

A quick smile, the chick goes to her station, and Wilson follows the rhythm of the announcer's last syllables and gives it up to his best friend and buddy, the black plastic square of lens hood and deep inside, the circular glass essence of the lens itself. Hates gameshows, loves that lens.

'And this here is the wheel of fortune itself. It's covered, as you can see, in various arcana, and why not?'

Now, that arcana bit wasn't on the autocue. Wilson could ad lib around that shit. He told himself it made it natural to do a bit of digressing here and there. Or maybe he was just showing off. Confusing the poor lady round the back of the set with her autocue machine on panic, and then dropping back into the official script just when it was on the edge. Yeah, showing off.

And he wasn't finished: 'The wheel has for centuries been used as a symbol for the vicissitudes of life. Boethius himself in his great work *The Consolation of Philosophy* compared history to a great wheel, hoisting you up and then dropping you down again.'

Up in the box the director and vision mixer exchanged weary looks. Their sense of resignation was positively Boethian.

The meat was on a roll: '"Inconstancy is my very essence," says the wheel. "Rise up on my spokes if you like but don't complain when you are plunged back down into the depths." The good times pass away but then so do the bad. Mutability is our tragedy and our hope. That is Boethius's wheel. If the cloud of unknowing, the mists that envelop us, were ever to clear, we'd see we're on a perfect wheel, and in an orderly motion that only seems chaotic. There is an ineluctability about the way we go up and then down.'

He'd gone too far, he'd strayed into Joyce, he'd lost the plot. Lost the studio audience way back. Change of pace, kid, change of pace.

A breath, the priest-like and slightly camp opening of the arms with hands held out, palm up and, 'So, let's spin that wheel!'

As the wheel span, his beginner's guide to medieval philosophy was undercut by the voices inside his head: 'OK, we'll just cut all that shit out, drop an audience shot from the ISO over the jump.' It was everyday stuff for them and it was in the earpiece for him. He always insisted on open talkback and he accepted their mildly amused sufferance.

But he wasn't finished. As the wheel slowed and the audience interest revived, he got back in his stride. Surely they want to know this – surely we can make this more than a quiz show?

'And after all's said and done, what is good and what is bad? Good fortune is dangerous. It can make you forget who you really are, what you really want. You can become the slave of success. The bad times, on the other hand, can set you free. That's when you find out who you really are. That's when you find out who your real friends are. Of course, if you fucked people over on your way up... Ohhh. Shit. Sorry, I swore, sorry guys.'

Groans from the gallery, shaken heads from the gentlemen on cameras, and a collective drawing-in of breath from the studio audience. Oh fuck, they're going hostile.

'That's alright Tony, we'll just do it again.' The director – patient, avuncular even.

Thank God for pity.

PART ONE

1
THE GREAT WINGS BEATING STILL

The twenty-five-year-old TV reporter was positively flying. Soaring. Floating.

Up in the Welsh mountains, he'd just strapped on a hang-glider. Make that he'd just strapped himself onto a hang-glider. It was cool. He'd had a two-minute run-through of how to do it from the guy who owned the thing, and the crew had now set up to film his maiden flight. Alright, run down this hill and you'll start to fly, then just grip the metal bar at the base of this triangle that meets up top in the great flapping wing. Push forward and you grab the wind, pull back and you pick up speed. Easy. And it wasn't like it was a cliff, like that bastard commando running last week. Made a real dick of himself. This was a gentle slope, getting steeper a hundred yards down, but presumably he'd be airborne by then…

▶▶▎

Meanwhile, and at exactly the same moment, in Piccadilly Gardens, the most unlovely commixture of cracked Tarmac and tired grass known to man, the centrepiece of the once great city of Manchester, two just-teens are feeding the pigeons.

Two kids – the taller, the elder, the leader, Shaun. Thirteen years of peculiar inputs had given him that sense of himself that Top Cat never lost. Younger brother, Paul, quieter, almost reserved, half his own man, half his brother's man.

'Look, it's eating it. Two of them. One named Peter, one named Paul, like you. Nibbley Dibbley Wing Ding, you know what I mean.'

Younger brother nodded. The elder's penchant for nonsense lyrics trawled from the further edge of seventies popular culture was a regular occurrence.

Pigeon Paul scoffs the breadcrumbs and the tiny crystals that are mixed in. After a moment, not even long enough to digest either the crumbs or what was happening to him, the 'loydel loydel' noise, the pigeon's purr, turns into a low shriek, wings flap madly and the pigeon sets off into the air and sky of downtown Manchester.

▶▶❘

And Wilson was rising into the Welsh air, a great gust had taken him up to 50 feet and he was absolutely getting the hang of it. Hang of it. Joke perhaps for the commentary after… shit… another gust caught him from the side. The great triangle was now veering madly to the left. A push forward only stalled the bastard and then another gust hit. The reporter and the contraption were now 100 feet off the floor, the hillside had become a precipice, but he wasn't flying into that, he was going rapidly sideways into the slope of the mountain at about 30mph. And it wasn't just hard earth, rocks and heather he was looking at having an experience with. There, parallel to his flight and now rushing towards him, was a barbed wire fence. Oh, God. This was more than bloody weasels to rip my flesh here.

The out-of-control 'flying machine' swooped towards the line of the fence.

At the last second, it whipped over the top and before relief could be experienced, smashed into the ground, Wilson's legs first, the great top strut of the hang-glider next. Bash. And then, ever so slowly, the wing tipped over on to its top. Pilot, man with broken ankle and newly lowered self-esteem, stuck in the straps, hanging, dangling, upside down. Swaying ever so slightly in what was left of the wind. Stuck. Looking like a dick. Again. And the camera crew. Did they rush down the hill to help? No. A nice slow zoom on their willing stooge, who had once again been hung out to dry.

▶▶❘

If he looked dumb, that's nothing to the pigeons. Squawking and insane fluttering at about 30 feet up was followed by a singular moment of peace and silence. As the poor fucking bird realized it was dead, or as good as. The silence was followed by the popping of the pigeon. The buggers just exploded and the carcass fell to earth, slamming into the hard urban ground of Manchester's 'Gardens'.

'Sassam, rassam, frassam, Rick Rastardly. Wing Ding forever and Amen,' intones young Shaun Ryder as he feeds the next candidate and watches him take wing.

'Here they come!' shouts Shaun as now half a dozen pigeons do the big grenade bit and crash to earth.

Two boys, as high on life as they will later be on other things, dance and laugh as feathers fall and skulls crack. They kick along the corpses like autumn leaves. The dead pass office windows, land on the plastic covers of babies' buggies; when passers-by put up their umbrellas, more pigeons impale and burst on the spikes. They fall in the canals. They fall on the estates.

'Grab him, nab him, shag him, shag him, stop that pigeon now.'

Thanks, Shaun.

Police records show that more than 3,000 pigeons were affected. They also show that this was the first arrest of the Ryder brothers. The first of many. And they also show that rat poison was mixed in with the bread-crumbs.

Jictar ratings showed that Wilson's 'Kamikaze' series, in which he did dangerous sports without any real training or preparation, and usually hurt himself, added a couple of points to the ratings for Tuesday night's magazine show here in the North-West of Little England. Injured leg, injured pride, people talking about you in the pub. That's the deal. Where do I sign?

▶▶▶

Wilson delivered the payoff piece to the 16mm camera: 'Well, I'm battered and bruised – I've done something rather unfortunate to my coccyx, I'm slightly upset and I'm utterly elated and I'll definitely be doing it again. This is Tony Wilson, a shadow of his former self, for *Granada Reports*, back to the studio.'

The camera stopped turning. 'Thanks a lot, I'm sure I'll be in touch, so excited love to do it again, cheerio.' His goodbye was courteous but brusque and of course utterly false; these fucking idiots had nearly killed him. Do it again? You must be fucking joking. He walked back down the hillside towards the humming city. Rather quickly.

piecetocam

Although there's a whole bunch of lies in this book – between the truth and the legend, print the legend (and we're all still arguing whether that's Howard Hawks, Liberty Valance or some other guy) – nevertheless, this last scene did actually happen.

Obviously, it's symbolic and it works on both levels.

I don't want to tell you too much, don't want to spoil the narrative.

But I'll just say 'Icarus'.

If you know what I mean, great; if you don't, it doesn't matter.

But you should probably read more...

2
GRANADALAND

England's North-West, the background to our little tale, is a bit like that bit of semi-desert between the Tigris and Euphrates in Iraq; a piece of land and a bunch of people that changed the world forever and then sank back into obscurity. In their aridity and poverty these places seem to pay the price for ever daring to kick evolution's arse.

At the dawn of civilization – that is, the invention of commercial television in the United Kingdom in the early 1950s – an entertainment entrepreneur from the East End of London got clever and bid for the Northern franchise; bid and won. For a while, Sidney Bernstein lorded it over both sides of the Pennines, the peat-moored spine of England, in both Lancashire and Yorkshire. Took a few years for the regulator to figure out that this much was too much, and by the sixties, Bernstein's territory, Granadaland, was just the western foothills reaching over to the Irish Sea. Manchester to Liverpool on the horizontal axis and junkie poet land in the North – the Lake District – down to Cheshire where the rich fuckers lived, and still do.

This was the land that gave us the modern world. This was the home of the Industrial Revolution, changing the habits of homo sapiens the way the agrarian revolution had done ten thousand years earlier. And what did that heritage mean? It meant slums. It meant shite. Burnt out by all that 'production'. Capital strides the globe and it walked out on this lot around the time Queen Victoria popped it. The remnants, derelict working-class housing zones, empty redbrick mills and warehouses and a sense of self that included loss and pride in equal if confused measures.

Quite a place and quite a TV company – named after Islamic Spain, who the fuck knows why. A commercial TV company. Loads of adverts. Yeah, commercial, but commercial like Warhol: 'I used to be a commercial artist, and then I just got more commercial.' Ratings, but with style. Populism underlaid with intellect and some serious socialist schtick. Left wing and commercial; God bless the presumption of dear Granada and its founder Lord Bernstein.

It went with the territory, or should we say, the region. A sense of being a bit above the other dicks in London or Birmingham. When Wilson arrived he had been given a speech by his head of department, a former Clydeside shop-steward turned documentary God, about how 'This was the company that brought Grierson and Eisenstein together in the thirties to cross-fertilize the new British documentary style with the inventor of modern cinema. And that's why you're not paid so much, you little bastards. You should be pleased we gave you a job.'

Please re-read the above with a Glaswegian twang and accept the guy's slightly dubious ship-builder background myth to understand why Wilson lapped it up. From the North himself, he had always felt a cut above too and was suddenly so at home. Here was an attitude that turned what might have been a chip on the shoulder into quality frites.

Today, though, he was restless; the hang-gliding special had gone out the previous night. The previous day he had filmed the next instalment; this one was waterski jumping – without training, and in mid-winter at Trentham Gardens Lake in Stoke-on-Trent. Drear, cold, and, with a decaying wetsuit that resembled a rubber string vest. Highly unpleasant. They had tried sixteen takes on the waterski jump but he'd fallen off and in on each one. It wasn't happening; they had a two-minute fast-cut pratfall sequence, but no more. In desperation and in failing light, a woman onlooker had offered her parachute from the back of a mud-splashed Range Rover and suggested a spot of parascending.

Five minutes later, he stood by the shivering black waters. Behind him two geezers held the parachute edges up in the air; ahead the thick rope tied to his waist snaked out over the water to a powerboat – a tragically underpowered powerboat – which was now setting off into the distance. 'Just wait till it pulls you off your feet, then run with it, after a couple of paces you'll go straight into the air...'

He was jerked hard forward and took a first step, then a second; now he was running, rope and boat to the fore and parachute dragging on the gravel bank behind him. 'Fuck, this is six paces and I'm not going uuuu-uuuuuppppp...' a trip and now he was on the ground. A cinematic back-ground allowed the immediate identification of a certain *Ben Hur* moment, or even *Ben Hur* momentum: being dragged along the ground, arms outstretched gripping rope, hanging on to horses and horsepower for grim death, and staring the same in the face.

To be precise, he was staring at a wooden jetty that stuck out from the grey sedge on the side of the lake. Irrelevant thirty seconds earlier, this jetty was growing in significance; and growing rapidly in size. The rope attached to the powerboat; yeah they've still got the throttle down, the rope is snaking over the jetty and its now about thirty yards away, Jeeesus it's the barbed wire fence all over again and now it's ten yards, aiiieeeeee.

At the very moment that wood and flesh were set to meld, a puff of air got into the nylon chute and Wilson's flailing body was pulled up out of the water, smashing across but not into the jetty, throwing him back down into the water on the other side, then suddenly getting the wind and lift-ing him straight up to 100 feet in the air. The motorboat crew suddenly realized they were dragging a piece of dead meat and cut the rope and, with the parachute not fully inflated, his body crashed back like a stone into the water. Just like that.

Think Icarus

▶▶▮

'Great show, Tony, loved the hang-gliding,' shouted one of the extras from *Hard Times*. Wilson waved back, managed a half-smile, and continued his forced march through the Granada backlot.

'See, it was fine. I don't know what you're worried about,' said Charles, head of regional programmes, a nice bloke who had happily turned an internal joke about getting Wilson to do films in which he just might die into a popular and much-talked-about-on-the-bus-the-next-morning Tuesday evening strand. Charles was a little overweight, red-brick and, well, a TV 'producer'. He would ascend the ladder. Wilson thought he loved TV a little too much; he didn't, he loved life, just thought TV was the same thing.

'No, no fucking way, I'm never doing another "Kamikaze" film, again. Ever.'

Wilson was on a roll. This was a twenty-five-year-old prima donna in full flow; it wasn't that he was a TV presenter and hence a minor celebrity in his home town. In fact, he had never intended celebrity. He had been shocked after his first few on-screen appearances to receive the typical scratchy illiterate fan letter including the obligatory 'this is a picture of me with my head inside your fly' kinda thing. Shocked. But this wasn't some newly found celeb stuff; he'd always had that prima donna edge from the age of eleven, when he filled in for Father Quinn on the Novena Rosary when the PP had laryngitis, and came first in the A stream in his first year at grammar school; Christmas, Easter and summer. He never looked back. Arrogant, not unpleasantly so, but then not pleasantly either. Right now he was indulging in that skill that never failed to amaze him in the cold light of hindsight; the ability to talk to his betters and bosses as if they were a piece of shit.

'How's the bird man of Derbyshire? Loved the hang-gliding, mate,' shouted a *Coronation Street* legend as Charles and his pissed-off presenter passed Studio 6.

'There, you see.'

'He doesn't have to deal with the consequences.'

'What consequences?'

'The possibility of death.'

Did Wilson take himself seriously? You bet your fucking life.

'Well, you're insured.'

'Is that meant to be a comfort? Never, Charles, never again.' (You stupid piece of shit.)

Round the corner came Razzer, Alan Erasmus, dressed as a nine-teenth-century Lascar. Afro seaman type. Alan was an actor and a hustler. Right now an extra in the network drama going on in Studio 12. His last speaking part was at the Chester Gateway a year back, but this was fair enough for the moment. He would get by. Alan would always get by. One of those human beings who float on life. Effortlessly.

'Hello, Charles,' said Alan. He waved an envelope at Wilson; it looked like he'd got tickets for a party or a football match.

'Al, tell him, the hang-gliding thing, wasn't it great? We got phone calls and everything. People liked it.'

'People, let me tell you,' interrupted Wilson, 'like public executions. Women get wet. I went to Cambridge. I am a serious person. I am a seri-ous fucking person living at one of the most serious fucking moments in human history, I mean it.'

'There's no need to swear,' said Charles to Wilson's receding back.

Charles had stopped walking, and Erasmus and Wilson continued. The debate about future programming was over for now. Serious moment in history? This was early 1976. Might as well have said 'one of the most depressing fucking moments in human history'. It was serious precisely 'cause it was so depressing.

Wilson was a child of the sixties, the late sixties. What happened? What the fuck happened? We had had Pope John 23rd, George Best, Martin Luther King, the Mini Moke and then topped it all off with music, drugs and marching in the streets. Yeah. And then the seventies. The Sheriff of Aspen was right. Stand on a hill outside Vegas and look west and you can see where the tide stopped and the reflux started. The night Ali lost to Frazier, says Thompson. That'll do. And now, it was Rick fuck-ing Wakeman, Slade and bands from Birmingham. Pomp rock and Pub rock and shite.

Fuck Fukyama; Pan's People were the end of history, not the collapse of the Berlin Wall. What do we want, we want thrilling; God made sex thrilling so we would fuck and procreate. And he knows how it goes down if anyone does. And Bob Dylan going electric and a charging student phalanx chanting 'Ho Ho Ho Chi Minh' and taking acid and driving to a war cemetery and turning out all the lights and listening to Jefferson Airplane's 'Volunteers' at screaming level on the day it came out and… these things were thrilling, and right then and there in the spring of 1976 Wilson was not being thrilled. And that was serious.

piecetocam

Ten years later, Liz Naylor, Manchester bisexual femme fatale and fat bird whose band was called The Gay Animals, would write of the mentors of the punk generation: 'It would be accurate to describe them as a bunch of still-born hippies from the tail end of an era which had trashed its promises and rather disappointingly fizzled out. Punk provided the perfect vessel for their thwarted ideas.'

Dead right, honey. We were a little bit stardust and a little bit fucking golden and some of us refused to believe that the Garden didn't exist. Once you've had a taste, you want more, don't you. Always. Yearningly. Isn't that the thrill jones? And anyway I gave you and your mate Cath two hundred quid to do Manchester's first colour photocopy fanzine and you fucked off with the money you made back, so fuck you.

Wilson and Erasmus have by now found their way into a darkened studio. All quiet except for the air con fans that will remove all evidence. They park themselves in a room set on a dilapidated sofa beneath an alpine mural that boasts some very nice porcelain ducks.

Alan is a mixed-race lad from Wythenshawe. Wythenshawe, the Projects in the country, seemed like a good idea at the time. Give them some grass; so their dogs can shit on it. Called Town Planning. Made it the biggest council estate in Europe back in the 1950s. And Erasmus was the only black kid. Twenty kids hit the local sweet shop – which one gets recognized? Jesus, no wonder Alan had developed an ease about life; he just had to. Like we said, he floated, one of those people who survive, thrive and make do without any visible form of support. Like there must be strings holding the fucker up, but the special-effects people have done this great job on hiding them. Invisible. Tough, trim, our Al had tight, curled hair already well on the way to grey.

And he was seriously eccentric, as in he was extremely serious about being eccentric. By the way, if you know Alan, one rule we all had was never lend him your car. But then if you know Alan, you'll already know that.

'Here we are, this is the best there is,' says Alan, reaching inside his shorts and producing a small, rounded piece of Lebanese gold with outer sacking still attached.

'You kept it in your jock strap. I'm not smoking something that's been in someone's jock strap.' Wilson screwed lips and nose in horror.

'Don't be daft, it was probably smuggled into the country wrapped in a condom and stuffed up someone's arse.'

'You see, this is my point. This is what we've come to. We are standing in Hilda Ogden's house smoking the contents of other people's arses. Not even people we know. There has to be more. There has to be more.'

3
THE MOVEMENT OF FREE TRADE

It's a hot night; it's been a hot day. Searing blue skies, kinda shade of blue you're not meant to get in this outpost of northern Europe. A heatwave was happening. Wilson had raced back from working in London for a gig.

The Free Trade Hall was just that. A massive construction hall in the centre of Manchester named after the city's successful contribution to the practical economics of the nineteenth century. Free Trade? Of course, there was nothing free about it. The bastards charged – a merchant is he who buys cheap and sells dear, be he gentile or Jew according to the sublimely quotable Jimmy Joyce. Maybe it meant they were free to charge what they wanted. Sounds a bit more Manc that way. Anyway, we invented the concept and now we called our hall after it. And the place had an iconic subtext. It was where we'd all gone to Speech Day. Any school worth its salt in our area had Speech Day at the Free Trade Hall and you'd get your prize – *Oxford Dictionary of Quotations* had been Wilson's favourite – on the same stage that on other nights would support the considerable weight of the Halle Orchestra, who themselves were supporting the considerable weight of expectation that one day they'd be a major world orchestra again.

But this wasn't exactly the gig for tonight. Tonight's gig was at the Lesser Free Trade Hall. Like getting non-specific urethritis. 'Lesser' and 'non-specific' seem such unnecessarily demeaning adjectives. But the Lesser it was. A small theatre way up in the top of the building. Looked like a local church hall. Set up for a capacity of 200 in floor-bolted seats that dated back to the forties. Needn't have worried. When Erasmus and

Wilson burst in to the desolate little theatre there were no more than forty or so people inside. Odd stragglers made their way in. Wilson didn't pay. He'd been invited.

He had a music show on TV, that's why.

For a decade and more, Granada had wanted to fuck the BBC by creating a rival to its Thursday night ratings-grabber *Top of The Pops*. The previous year, when Wilson had attempted to get himself in studio as a presenter instead of on the road as a reporter, he and his mates had created a small, perfectly formed fifteen-minute arts show that featured the odd band as well as pissing llamas and a bastard comedian called Bill Oddie who hit Wilson over the head very hard with a copy of *The Goodies Christmas Annual 1975* and damn near knocked him out with forty more live seconds to the hand-over. (Bastard.)

Wilson's bosses wondered whether they could convert this little slot into Independent Television's *TOTP*-fucker. Turned out no way, but they gave it a run-out. And the news that that geezer off the local telly was going to do a music show, revealed in a small news story in the *New Musical Express*, provoked the first intimations for Wilson that the world had not died. That God had not just fucked off.

The First Sign. It began at Christmas as drear '75 rolled into drear '76. A dear junkie friend from Cambridge, Dead-head and antiquarian book seller, gave him a copy of this new album by that New York poetess chick – Christ, I remember her, she had done the voice-over for 'Robin Having His Nipple Pierced'. The album was called *Horses*. It was wonderful. It was like something from another planet.

Stretford *is* another planet. It is a suburb of a suburb. It put the semi in semi-detached. Yes, it houses the greatest football team in the world, and his granny lived there, but Wilson wasn't going to get excited about Stretford or a brown cardboard packet postmarked from Stretford. But this was the Second Sign. Said packet contained a battered album sleeve, no album, just the sleeve, by a band Wilson had never heard of, The New York Dolls, and a letter:

Dear Mr Wilson,

I heard you are doing a new music show. Please can we have more bands like this.

Yours,

Stephen Morrissey (aged fourteen)

And shortly thereafter, the Third Sign.

A cassette. A C45, Malcolm, a Cfucking45. On the card liner:

Dear Mr Wilson,

This is a tape by a new band from London, who I think you should like. I am arranging a gig for them at the Lesser Free Trade Hall in early June and hope you can come.

Yours,

Howard Trafford

The three songs on the cassette were loud, raucous, intriguing. New. It was in the diary. It was time.

4 June, 1976. Lesser Free Trade Hall. People dotted around. Desultory. Strange.

A thin, handsome mekon appeared on the small proscenium stage. 'Hi, we're the Buzzcocks but we're not ready yet, so we're not playing tonight, but this is the Sex Pistols.'

A band emerged. Who knows what the drummer, bass player and guitarist looked like. The guy who took centre stage took the mike, took your mind. A swagger to make John Wayne look a pussy. A sneer so dismissive of everyone and everything, of God and civilization, in just one pair of twisted lips. And then they started playing.

Twenty-five years on, Britain's top commercial/art filmmakers made a movie about this evening. To explain the impact on the twentieth century of this seminal gig, they had people like Wilson and Erasmus pogoing towards the end. That's called filmmaking, and who gives a toss about truth. How do you explain that no one moved, no one budged?

piecetocam

4 June 1976. The Sex Pistols play Manchester for the very first time. There are only forty-two people in the audience but they are all dazed, in shock and absorbing the energy on which they are all starting to feed; on power, on energy and magic. Inspired, they will go forth and perform wondrous deeds.

Over there at the back is Howard Devoto and Pete Shelley; they organized the gig, they're miles ahead of everybody in Manchester, they're already the Buzzcocks.

Across the aisle; two young lads from Salford Grammar School, Bernard Sumner and Peter Hook, soon to become Stiff Little Kittens, then Warsaw, then Joy Division and finally New Order.

The little ginger nut, that's Mick Hucknall.

And there's the Stretford school kid, Morrissey.

That's Jon the Postman; he's a postman.

And there, mad professor eyes under hippy haircut, the town's wannabe producer and knob twiddler: Martin Hannett, one of the true geniuses in this story.

He will later want to kill me.

They stared, open-mouthed, transported to a place where you didn't need to pogo (it wasn't invented till three months later). That place was real life; that place was the clearing in the undergrowth where meaning and elucidation live, that place was the place where music came from and the place it would take you back to.

But they knew nothing, these forty-odd strangers, gathered by chance and chat, they just knew their world would never be the same again. A past obliterated and No Future.

This blur of noise, it was fucking loud, and the snarling vocal emotion gave no clue to what it was, other than that it was something unutterably special. For Wilson, stunned, historically relieved, transported and completely confused, it was the seventh number that opened with some faint familiarity.

'God, what the fuck is this? Bloody hell, it's "Stepping Stone".' And in the next sixty seconds, hearing the Pistols violently murder and then resurrect this simple pop classic, all was made clear as all was destroyed. Only in hearing the old was the new revealed. I will destroy the temple and in three minutes I will rebuild it, sayeth the Lord, sayeth Johnny Rotten. Clarity for the one academic arsehole in the audience. The tune, the song, the lyrics, the beat of this Monkees gem were assailed with utter confidence, utter anger. In its complete indifference to the niceties of technique and respect, they restored to the popular song the spirit that is the only fucking reason it exists in the first place. Robert Johnson sold his soul at the crossroads. He sold it for this. Good deal. At last.

Wilson and his mate Alan left speedily. The man in the black leather jacket and black leather trousers, Malcolm, the seller of black leather trousers, asked him what he thought.

'Amazing; but the Pete Townsend stuff...' referring to guitarist Jones's boiler suit and wheeling guitar arm.

'Yeah, yeah it's going.'

Out into the hot dark night. And his and every other bastard's destiny.

4
LATER THAT SAME NIGHT

Razzer and Wilson were, as advertised previously, children of the sixties. The late sixties. Second generation. Razzer's flat, however, was a bastard of the fifties. A two-bedroom place in a three-storey 1920s pile; the age of architectural invention was buried in the décor, early fifties brown. Brown wallpaper, brown furniture, brown carpet. Worn brown carpet; yes, that peculiar shade of brown that is quite simply 'worn'.

And the locale; that suburb of Manchester called Didsbury. A unique commixture of the exotic about three miles south of the city; one part mid-level professional, one part reform Jewish, one part muso-drug dealer (the ones that hadn't left town for the moors above Hebden Bridge – why acid casualties should have upped sticks to hang out with Sylvia Plath's corpse was always a mystery to literary student Wilson, but there you have it) with a couple of council estates on the side; extra flavouring you could take or leave.

Midnight. Erasmus looked with slight affection at the *Dark Side of the Moon* poster taped to the wall. 'Must go.' And with a slight hint of the violence that had dripped in from Rotten's performance, ripped said relic from the wall and screwed it up.

He moved inexorably left. Face to face with Bowie.

'Not David,' said Lindsay. Wilson's girlfriend/wife. Think Audrey Hepburn. The adjective that does the job is 'gamine' – think it, imagine it. The only adjective appropriate to a young woman whose tight buttocks fit jeans in a way that is... appropriate. They'd got married to see if the rows would stop. They didn't. Tonight was reasonably mellow, though, as a result of the Thai green. She cracked the last of it off the imported tooth-pick. Scattered it in the Number 10 and pleaded again: 'Not David, Alan.'

'Fuck him; he goes.'

The poster came easily off the wall; connections to the past few years were as tenuous as the curled-and-yellowing Sellotape that held the Diamond Dog to the flock wallpaper.

The two boys were brooding; not talking about what had happened, but letting it sink in, accompanied, of course, by the marijuana. How far they were from the speed and alcohol culture that they were inadvertently embracing was easy to see from their dress; Erasmus was relatively cool and casual, but Wilson's tie-dye T-shirt and scarf, a knotted silk scarf for fuck's sake, belied the clarion call of history. And it wasn't just the tie-dye; it was the dope too. Their generation had grown up and away; Dead-head stickers on Cadillacs and the rest. As the drear seventies dragged on, serious dope smoking became a relic of times past. Erasmus and Wilson refused to move on; these were guys who never got drunk, while all about them... Just not their drug.

'It's really good stuff, isn't it,' said Lindsay.

'It is good, where do you get it from Al?'

'A mate of mine brought it back from his holidays.'

'The Caribbean?'

'Rhyl, the Sun Centre Rhyl.'

'Right...'

5
AND SO IT GOES

The next morning, Peter Hook went into Mameloks music shop on Oxford Road and said to the man: 'Please can I have a bass guitar.' The man took one down from the wall. 'Thank you,' said Peter. 'How much is that?'

'Thirty-five pounds.'

'Thank you,' said Peter, again. He gave the man the cash and walked out of the shop with his own personal instrument.

He admits today he had no idea why he did this; he just did it.

Wilson was a mite more self-conscious of his job and of the deep responsibilities placed on him by history and location. He went to work and then he went to work; he burst into Charles's office. It was to become a tiresomely repetitive litany:

'I've seen a band, an absolutely amazing gig last night, we have to put them on the show. They have a bad reputation but we have to have them on.'

'Give me one reason, one good reason,' answered Charles, who frankly had more important things on his mind.

'I would describe last night as history.'

'How can you describe it as history? There was hardly anybody there.'

'What difference does that make? How many people were at the Last Supper?'

'Twelve. Thirteen if you count Jesus.'

'Well, there you go. How many people were at the murder of Julius Caesar?' continued Wilson, realizing his cheap historic analogies were annoying his immediate boss and making the profound point that he, Wilson, understood these things and must be trusted, believed and consented to.

'I don't know, Tony, you tell me.'

'Five. So shut up. You coming with me to ask the big chief?'

'No.'

'Good, I'll do it myself.'

Wilson entered the viewing theatre; there he was, inspecting one of his high-budget dramas, Lord Bernstein, founder of Granada Television.

It has to be said that Wilson's scorching disrespect for immediate superiors was only matched by the grease and unctuousness with which he treated big bosses. And this was the Big boss.

He sat down two seats away – respect, respect – and throughout the ensuing conversation assisted his argument with a TV presenter's hand movements. Here, sir, I'm explaining something very important to you and very dear to me, so I'm pulling it out of my heart, sir, with these very hands. Bollocks, but it usually works.

'Excuse me, sir, I have a rather important request. For you, sir, for Granada to put on a rather controversial band called the Sex Pistols.'

'What exactly is a Sex Pistol?' replied the old gentleman.

'The BBC have banned them, sir, town councils have banned them, bloody British Rail have banned them, sir. This is Manchester, I believe we do things differently here.'

'I'm told they do a song about the Queen.'

'Yes and they also do a song called "Anarchy in the UK".'

'Anarchy, my father was an anarchist, nothing wrong with a bit of anarchy.'

piecetocam

Was it Lord Bernstein that pivotal morning? Maybe not, but the traditions of the left-wing peer's commercial TV station were what let it go through; getting the Pistols on telly; piss easy at this Northern dream factory.

The day of the Pistols on Wilson's show was not that easy.

The group arrived in Reception at the Granada building and proceeded to lie on the floor instead of sitting in the chairs provided. Rotten lay on the marble steps that led to the first floor, right under a Bacon 'Screaming Pope'; fuck the Pope and fuck Francis Bacon. He didn't notice. And anyway, there was more art in the way the boy lay there than in the twisting, turning Prelate above.

In the Green Room, the group picked a row with the show's co-presenter, the radical critic-comic Clive James. And their roadie, a crazed young woman called Jordan, was sporting a swastika arm band. During rehearsal, Wilson was called to the box; 'Sort it' said Charles; this is a bleeding Jewish company.

Wilson intervened; the past negotiating with the future. The answer as to so many other problems in the twentieth century – gaffer tape.

And then the moment came:

Wilson came to the last act of, the last episode of, the first series of *So It Goes*.

On the monitors behind Wilson, the words 'MORE MINIMALISM'; the image, in Jean Luc Godard's immortal words, fucking the presenter from behind.

'Finally, tonight, one of the most reviled phenomena of recent weeks, the Sex Pistols, you can hear them warming up...'

What a shit phrase 'warming up' – if that wasn't enough, being announced by this TV stick insect in his all-denim outfit, patched jeans and fitted denim shirt, was just too much for the band and before Wilson got the 'up' out of the corner of his mouth, Jones had smashed his first bar-chord and Lydon had started to scream-drawl the ominous intonation: 'Woooooordstooock... coming to geeeert yer... get off your fucking arse.'

And wham, 'Anarchy in the UK' launches at full pelt.

The impact of that first night at the Lesser Free Trade Hall was now being hurled down approximately one million cathode ray tubes. In the two months since the Free Trade Hall, it wasn't just the Townsend impersonation that had gone; everything had tightened into a pure electric charge. And they'd written this song. Fuck. Chuck Berry may have advanced the cause of R&B literature by naming specific makes of automobile, but these boyos were discussing 'council tenancies'. Oh, yes, oh yes.

Their slot was three and half minutes; they played six and half minutes because they needed the last three to kick shit out of the set. The show was edited for transmission. On the good side, it means that on archive shows you get these incredible slow-mos of John staring, scarily into the middle distance; that's the audience he's staring at. With eloquent hate. As if he wants every single onlooker to just fuck off and die...

You could tell people not to stand in the doorway or block up the hall. Or you could give 'em the Lydon look and politely suggest they just fuck off and die.

The bad news was that the post-production scam allowed the bosses to dub a little mild applause over the end of the song as the feedback echoed out.

Lost forever, the sound of history being made; the absolute and empty silence with which the 300-odd 'music fans' in the studio audience greeted the Sex Pistols' inaugural TV outing. Silence, complete, deafening.

Except for the sound of feet clanging on the metal stairs down from the control box. Charles on his way to punch these bleeders for trashing his set.

By the time he got to the studio floor, the group were long gone – a quick getaway proving that a background in petty thievery comes in handy sometimes.

And Wilson. A grin, almost like Brian Jones's when the audience and police riot at each other across the stage of a Stones gig and the main man crouches behind a speaker, grinning like the serpent when Eve goes for the apple. Wilson was grinning and lest we think that his intro had shown commendable restraint and even good taste; he did have a final word or two to camera before the credits rolled to Dobie Gray's 'Gimme the beat, boys...'

'Bakunin would have loved it.'

Did he really say that?

Pretentious git, but useful in certain ways.

6
CONCERNING ELVIS COSTELLO AND ELVIS PRESLEY

That was the end, the end of the first series of *So It Goes*. The team were told that they had a recommission, for the following autumn.

Shooting apples in a barrel, punching a suspect in the stomach when your colleagues have his arms pinioned, blowing people away when they're buried up to their chins in hot sand; we're looking for another way of saying 'piss easy'. That's what series two of *So It Goes* felt like. First there was a nervous spring and summer; surely somebody else in British TV would figure that this was Merseybeat all over again, the shot in the arm, amphetamine only, that we had unconsciously cried for. This was another dawn of high pop art. They should have slept easy, Wilson and his TV cronies; like Butch Cassidy they had vision and the rest of the world were wearing bifocals... The involuntary blindness of British mainstream media had fallen for the same old degenerative crap; the idea that art is technique and technique is art.

For Christ's sake.

The geezers who ran the BBC's music empire, whose pinnacle was the lame-as-fuck *Old Grey Whistle Test*, were nice enough guys. But they didn't like punk because the bands couldn't play their instruments. Nice one, guys.

Let's just say Andrea Del Sarto. If you get it, fine. If you don't, that's OK. But maybe you should read more.

Steve Wells, the *NME* journalist who began the destruction of the Happy Mondays with a deftly spun two-page spread accusing the shock-monsters from Salford of homophobia put it nearly as well as Browning. Expressing disgust and moral loathing at Jools Holland joining Paul Weller on stage at some festival, his prose screamed 'For God's sake, keep musicians away from pop music.'

In fact, it was precisely the inability to play that gave the tonal freshness to the angry rant of punk rock. If you could play the guitar in those days, you played C, F and G7, or E, A and B7. That's how you learned. With your maroon mock leather guitar bag and those Joan Baez, David Bowie dreams.

Little did you know, rebellious youth, you were being constrained, controlled, hand-cuffed; held tight in the melodic restriction of the 1-4-5 tonal system. Fuckers. Some men rob you with a six gun and some with Western tonal systems. Bert Weedon had you by the balls.

But *punk*. Just fucking hit it, son... And if knowing three chords is too much, which it is, if 'learning things' isn't on your to-do list, then know just one, just one chord. It's an F shape, and how fucking appropriate that it should be an F. And you just run it up and down that fretboard. Go anywhere, up and down, whatever feels right and makes you and your mates jump up and down. For a shade of emotion, move a bit of your first over a string and you have a go-anywhere B minor. However, the point of these technicalities is that no one except this thin, tubercular-looking kid living near Erasmus in Didsbury knew anything about technicalities, and anyway, Vini Reilly hasn't made his appearance yet.

And the sad fucks who ran the British Broadcasting Corporation believed in God-almighty technique; that or an American passport. So the BBC politburo turned their back on the new talent and come the summer of '77, the field was clear for Wilson and his pals at Granada to put the new music on the telly. In the interim, they'd done the Buzzcocks on the local news show, badum badum. And invited a kid up from London to play a song called 'Everything is Less Than Zero'. The lad arrived; no band, just a guitar and amp. 'Excuse me, I wrote another song last week, can I play that instead?'

33

'Go ahead, whatever you fancy.'

And the teatime TV viewers of England's North-West were treated to a perfect modern love song in which some poor fucker gets his fingers cut off, and they're left lying in a wedding cake.

Yes, yes, yes. Post-modern Buddy Holly geezer gives great song to the North-West tea-time viewers. Say hello to Elvis Costello.

See what I mean; piss easy.

The precious few at the Lesser Free Trade Hall had become an overexcited little community. Every week brought a great new song, a great new talking point, and a gig or two at the former metal venue, the Electric Circus, which had opened its urine-stained stairway to every new 'punk' band in the land. Come the summer of '77, and plans were laid for the autumn series. No more studio bands; Wilson would do the links from studio, a bank of black-and-silver-lined monitors, but that was it. The performances would come from the venues, the new churches of this sacramental music.

Best night was 16 August. That *was* the Circus. 'Don't gob at me,' said Pete Shelley, with pleasant familiarity, and the accent on 'gob', to the swaying, leaping mob; and launched into 'Orgasm Addict'; first-time round bass player Hoss, their connection with the people, swayed and arched backwards.

Magnificent – as were the Jam from London and Penetration from up there in the North-East. Wilson and his team had a cameraman on either side of stage, and the entire crew had been issued lightweight anoraks.

Jon the Postman, a postman, had developed the habit of leaping onto Manchester stages at the end of a gig and leading the throng in a violently a cappella rendition of 'Louie Louie', the old Kingsmen classic.

It was an age when ceremony was abandoned as bogus and rotten, and with encore and unlikely politeness, this closing choral event was most welcome. That night at the circus the Postman went on overtime. Wilson went on stage to encourage him off. Spat on? Drenched.

Midnight, back at the Granada car park, the man at the Lodge told the returning camera cars the news. Elvis had left the auditorium. Fucker was dead. A kind of moment. Kind of serious. This revolt wasn't against him. He'd been a punk; still was in the obese nihilism of his closing years. But it was a moment; like the leaves of a calendar fluttering through a forties black-and-white movie; time passes, it comes and goes.

The Clash at Belle Vue was a riot. Just that, a riot. Fuckers arrived three hours late for the sound check, brought some mates whom Wilson and his team hadn't booked; some girl in strange white make-up. Suzie or Siouxsie or something – fine, if you say this lot are cool, we'll film them too, but get your fucking gear unloaded cause there's 1,000 people standing outside in the rain and they're going to smash the fucking windows in.

They did.

Iggy too was special; he'd visited Manchester the previous year, side-stage for a Bowie whom punk had now sidestaged.

Back at the Apollo in September 1977, he was possessed and at the height of his powers. During 'Lust for Life' the daddy of punk surged to the audience barriers; people surged to him, bouncers pushed and punched them back, Iggy squirmed and held the mike high and twisted it downward, pointing at the action, wanting the thing itself, the hysteria, to join in the mix. During 'The Passenger' he sat on the front of the stage, and delivered some of his rap straight to the *So It Goes* camera, later confiding to Wilson, 'Hey, who was that cameraman – he danced with me, he fucking danced with me.' The performance was extraordinary. Confessing to the audience, mid-'Passenger', that he'd met a girl called Lucille in Amsterdam and that he'd asked her if she liked Cadillacs and she'd said, 'Iggy I hate fucking cars.' Good line, and it was to cause problems in Wilson's relationship with the big G. But before we get to that, reality check.

piecetocam

In reporting these events to the movie-going public, the final band shown in a quick run-through of So It Goes *stars are the Stranglers. This takes no account of the fact that Wilson hated*

*these old men who were, in his frequently voiced opinion, band-
wagon jumpers, jumping on punk like the Police would jump New
Wave a few months later. He threatened to not present the show
featuring them, refused to go to some shitty London venue to film
them. Moaned like fuck, and despite making life a misery for a
couple of weeks for those around him, failed completely to block
them from the series. We insert this fact-flash not just to get
matters straight, but to illustrate how we could be accused of
describing Wilson as some kind of gestalt Napoleon, while in fact
the little General was part of a team and frequently got overruled.*

▶▶▌

Cut to two young kids watching telly with their dad.

The dad is Derek, Derek Ryder, a remarkable man who brought up two
remarkable children, though the really remarkable human in all this is
Mrs Ryder – 'Oh, my two silly sons.' The Ryders will figure later, and
significantly, in our history. They scorn, as did their impresario-to-be
Wilson, these MOAPs, these disordered pensioners.

The Stranglers cavorting and gurning on the TV screen.

'They're shit.'

'We'll have no fucking swearing in this house,' says their dad.

You see what I mean.

Anyway, the music these two precocious children liked was beyond
varied. If they could have spelt eclectic, they would have had it tattooed
on their foreskins. And their dad's broad spectrum, voluminous record
collection and starry-eyed enthusiasms played their part. Eclectic? He
had Karl Denver records, a northern pop-singer from the late fifties-early
sixties who gave the world its first full-on version of 'Wimoweh'.

'Now that's music,' says the elder kid.

And years later, Karl and the two boys Shaun and Paul worked together
on a few songs.

7
I HATE F**KING CARS

Wilson was hauled into the big boss's office at the big G. It was a couple of weeks since the rows raged over Iggy Pop using the word 'fuck' mid-song. The big boss wanted it cut. The little bossy boots that was Wilson fought like fuck for art, art that seemingly only he understood or valued. And Iggy's lyrics were art and inviolable.

One can understand the pain of having to hear this stuff treated as art. With the similarity between cutting a four-letter word out of a diatribe by a semi-naked lunatic from Detroit and removing a chorus from a Mozart aria utterly lost on the big boss, Wilson had lost the battle and was forced to get some audience noise to swell up and drown out the 'fucking' and then drop back again just as quickly. To this day, devotees of La Osterberg wonder what had happened at the Apollo that night to make the audience go 'Ooooohhhh' in such a way.

It's an Iggy pop quiz question: 'Why did the audience ooooooh at the Manchester Apollo in 1977?'

And since we're getting educational on your ass, let's have a Martin Scorsese pop quiz too. Who's the guy in the back of shot in the long café conversation scene in *King of Comedy* who keeps waving and smiling at the camera while Pupkin explains his plans and dreams to girlfriend Rita?

The answer?

Isn't it enough that you now know why the audience noise comes and goes three minutes into 'The Passenger' in one of the most riveting filmed versions of this Osterberg classic? And you also know half the reason for the premature end of *So It Goes*. The Iggy fuck-problem had not gone away. The show itself was recorded 'as for live', to go out half an hour later. The film of the offending song came and went, impressively if mysteriously. Wilson said goodnight and handed over to the closing song that would run into the credits: 'Lust For Life'.

By mistake, a little over-eager, and still a bit pissed with losing the battle, he shortened his outro. Not like him, many thought. So the song was left to play for an extra fifteen seconds. It had been cut to fade out at the first whiff of applause; now it went on the few extra seconds. And there, clear as a bell, loud as a belch, just before the mix to the Granada Blue. Iggy. Shouting at the top of his voice:

'Clap your FUCKING hands!'

Ooooops.

'I want to make this very clear. That is the last show of the last series. If I ever see that man with the horse's tail coming out of his arse again you will be fired.' This reference to Iggy's 'interesting' onstage attire was the death knell. No argument was needed. Exit stage left. These people paid him; they could tell him what to do. It was simple economics and Wilson retreated, tail uncomfortably nestled between legs.

▶▶|

While Wilson and his TV cronies had been hard at work exposing the late-night UK TV-watcher to the delights of the new music, Erasmus had got his hands really dirty. He had started managing a band. A relatively tame bunch of lads, just a local band by the name of Flashback. Yep, that bad. Razzer gave them a new name, Fastbreeder, which was hardly any better, but they had energy and spirit, and at least Alan was now in the game.

Nine months in, on 24 January 1978, Alan rang his mate to say he'd been sacked in a midnight coup. A couple of second-generation Didsbury hippies who wanted a punk gig moved in, sacked the drummer and rhythm guitarist. And manager Alan. Their mates were the new managers. Al was out.

Wilson, on that very day, was digesting the end of his TV music career; a return to straight reporting, even heavy politics, was OK to a point, but he had, through his job, come close to the stuff of his dreams. Malcolm

McLaren had given him a naked boy Sex Pistols T-shirt, Elvis Costello, who despised the media except the ones who had been kind to him early, nodded a hello in Wilson's direction as he went on stage for a major gig. What had seemed to be his passionate hobby had become, for those two years, a part of his real life. He had touched his dream world, connected, and now his fingers were being cut off.

Only one thing to do on the day that Razzer phoned him. Join up. Join up. He rang Razzer back and told him to go round and see the guitarist and drummer and tell them not to give up; they'd start another band. And Erasmus and Wilson would co-manage. Hurrah. One of those moments, one of those days.

The first job was to get in other members. Erasmus had an idea – there was this guitarist who lived round the corner. Had played in the odd punk band, which was particularly bizarre since the kid was a virtuoso. No, not technical proficiency stuff. We're talking the Tortellier of the Fender Strat. It's not technique when a human brain and a sound wave projecting piece of wood-and-metal become one transmitting device. Virtuoso.

A meeting was arranged. The day before, Wilson had an ominous phone call from a mate who had managed the kid before. 'How can you have a guy in a band who sends doctors' notes to say he can't make rehearsal, two weeks in advance? He's a complete mind-fuck.'

Undeterred, encouraged in fact by the idea of the deeply unbalanced genius, Erasmus and Wilson visited the genius in his girlfriend's dad's house, where he was living at that particular moment.

Vini Reilly had the face of an angel. Thin, white, emaciated and probably touched by God. Anorexic body shape and exaggeratedly angular fingers and brain.

He was the one who explained the liberating effect of the rampant bar chord on the formalism of late twentieth century popular music.

He was in.

8
IDIOT WIND

Erasmus and Wilson were a team. The reefer madness that had brought them together in an era when dope was going out of fashion for every-body else, declining into the salad days of their late twenties, now fuelled a partnership.

Nights out on the town were predictable. The low-level but surprisingly vehement disparagement that the local public of English cities reserve for their local half-stars always served as overture.

'Wanker.'

'Thank you,' almost meant, as Wilson, Lindsay and Razzer moved past the Rafters talent-night queue towards the door.

Rafters was a long established basement club right in the city centre and in the aftermath of the punk explosion had cornered the market for putting on New Wave that was on its way up the shore. Driftwood and treasure appeared in equal proportions.

'Tosser.'

'Very original,' replied Wilson, who just kept moving.

Alan didn't; almost turned to have a pop at one of the 'fans': 'How does he put up with this?'

'He loves it; says he doesn't care whether it's applause or boos, just the volume that counts.' Lindsay said this in a resigned fashion. Ambivalent about her partner's ego. Hates it and loves it.

Wilson did say that 'volume counts' line fairly often, like most of his 'theories'. He had taken this one from the temple of his childhood, the Royal Shakespeare Theatre in Stratford-on-Avon. His former actor dad and his up-for-a-night-out-even-if-it's-a-mission-at-Mulberry-Street mum liked theatre and Wilson had been dragged smiling to Stratford since the early sixties.

The plays were good, but in those days when Best was best and the past was set in stone to become golden, the programmes that went with the RSC were honey-pits of wit and words; great quotes from all over the bloody place that referred directly or incredibly indirectly to the piece about to be performed. This one, it's the volume that counts, may have been an Oscar Wilde. The fount lost in time, but not the gist.

And as a line it was great to shore against the mob.

At the end of the queue was a fan. Jesus. Outnumbered eight to one, but it made the passage passable.

'Can I have your autograph, Tony?'

'Sure.'

Wilson was attentive and kindly to the fan. There was generosity here. There was also pity. Secretly, he was on the side of the 'wanker faction'. Anyone wanting his autograph and displaying such weakness in public was just a little short of the Right Stuff and therefore elicited polite, even serious concern on the part of the minor celeb.

The trio passed through the doors of Rafters and headed down the staircase to the long, low-slung basement. Hardly down the stairs when a girl with a punky look accosted Wilson with one of those 'what can I say to this person off television' openers.

'When's *So It Goes* coming back, then? We can get up a petition to bring it back.'

Before he could get out an empty response, a voice spat out from the DJ box that nestled on the stair landing: 'He doesn't want it to come back. He wants it to be gone forever. Then it can grow into a legend.'

Wilson was taken aback. Such wit and wisdom from a member of the public. With an expansive hand gesture to the large figure looming out of the back of the box, Wilson welcomed an equal into his life and explained to the girl, 'There you have it, a man with a true grasp of semiotics. There's your answer, sweetheart.'

'Can I buy you a half?' smiled Wilson to Mr Intelligent Member of the Viewing Public.

But this was no member of the public. This was Wilson's future.

'You can buy me a pint.'

As much taken aback by the forward-looming physicality of this new mate as he was by the doubling of the drinks order, Wilson smiled. It wasn't just stumbling across bands that filled his life, it was stumbling across people. This one. Who knows?

The name of the Rafters DJ that night was Robert Gretton. Sorry, Robert Leo Gretton. Like Erasmus, he was from Wythenshawe; like Wilson he was direct grant Catholic grammar school, though Rob's alma mater was St Bede's in Whalley Range, famed for Peter Noone and legendary folk comedian and eco-terrorist Mike Harding, who would like it to be known that his school also accommodated great left-wing playright Trevor Griffiths (as well as the drummer in Freddie and the Dreamers), whose role in British culture's first true piece of post-modernism will necessarily go undiscussed in this book.

This is hardly in the same league as the great novelist Anthony Burgess, who went to the Catholic Grammar School, Xaverian, in Rusholme. This was the old school of Martin Hannett, and though you haven't met Martin yet, you will, and we couldn't pass over this alma mater bit without mentioning Anthony Burgess and the fact that his real name was Anthony Wilson.

If you haven't read *Earthly Powers*, it doesn't matter. But you should probably read more.

Wilson didn't go to either of these noble institutions. He was a De La Salle boy from Salford. And his school hero was Terry Eagleton, Marxist literary critic whom Wilson revered and constantly referred back to.

But for Bede's and Robert Leo Gretton, it was Peter Noone. Perhaps we should remember that Herman's Hermits were the biggest band in the world back in 1965. Or perhaps we should try and forget.

Gretton had worked in an insurance office. Hated it.

Gretton had been part of the Wythenshawe industrial mafia – which meant working in baggage-handling at Manchester Airport, the best job in post-industrial Lancashire.

Despite the pool table and TV and employee conditions that would have shamed a Japanese multinational, he hated it.

He wanted excitement and music. Somewhere, there is a photograph of Rob in a tassled Travolta-esque all-in-one, swirling on a Northern Soul dance floor. Music. Rob wanted music. In his life. Of his life. And wore bloody tassles to show it till it became blackmail material.

That's one reason why he had wangled the DJ job that night.

'Hey can you play some Cure, mate?'

'Cure for what, sticky-up hair?'

'No, the Cure, mate. The group.'

'I don't play no London shite. Fuck off.'

And then again, tonight was dual purpose. Rob had just started managing a local band who were due to play that night. Like Wilson, he had seen them when they were an outrageous noise-filled mess called Warsaw. A four-piece that grew out of that same Pistols gig we all attended earlier. At exactly the moment Wilson was haranguing his Granada bosses to get the Pistols on telly, Peter Hook had bought that bass guitar. History had been calling.

He was starting a group. Warsaw.

They were everything that Pistols night had promised. Untrained, and pure aggressive noise. And a shit name. Gretton had approached the guitarist Barney in a phone box in central Manchester. Did they want a manager? Yes. The rest is not silence.

piecetocam

In attempting to describe Mr Gretton, who is indeed a central character in this epistle, I think it's best to go back to the early attempts of those filmmakers we've been mentioning to capture his spirit. With a blithe and almost rebellious attitude to the world market for their upcoming epic, the writer, director and producer of 24 Hour Party People *had captured Robert Leo Gretton with the sublime epithet: 'a cross between Bradley Hardacre and Andy Warhol.'*

Oh, fucking yes. Unspeakably accurate.

There's a phrase, 'Will it play in Omaha?' and it's important to know that the first modern multiplex was built in Omaha, Nebraska. Will it work in the US multiplexes? 'A cross between Bradley Hardacre and Andy Warhol' probably wouldn't work in the UCI in Sheffield on a wet Friday night.

Fuck 'em. Much as Rob would have.

Bradley Hardacre was a comic-book, larger-than-life, nine-teenth-century Lancashire industrialist, who was funny, brutal and utterly self-possessed.

Andy Warhol? Well, you should read more.

9
HERE ARE
THE YOUNG MEN

'You cunt.'

Wilson and Gretton were making friends with each other at the bar. Erasmus was playing pool with Lindsay.

'You fucking cunt.'

A scrawny young lad, at the other side of the pool table. Intense, intense eyes. And a voice on him.

'You're a fucking cunt.'

'Interesting opinion,' answered the local celeb. 'Is he a friend of yours?' to Gretton, who was leaning sideways on the bar.

'He's our lead singer,' said Gretton.

As his lead singer moved past the pool table towards the bar, Wilson recognized the crazed frontman from Warsaw. Ah, yes.

Ian Curtis stopped his advance a few inches short of Wilson's nose. Never one for violence, of any sort (complete bloody wimp since primary school) Wilson shrank into himself.

'Do you think he's going to hit me?'

Gretton let the question hang in the air. Gretton was the impeccable personal terrorist. He liked 'situations' and his lead singer was putting the TV man into a situation.

A silence, then a phrase.

'You cunt.'

'Yes, you've said that.' A little sarcasm was restoring Wilson's *sang froid*.

'The shit you put on telly and you don't put us on. You fucking cunt.'

Wilson was about to explain that there were limited slots, that there was a queue, but that in fact he had already thought that the next band he should slot into his *Granada Reports* music collection was the Warsaw lot. But excuses and promises dried up as the staring eyes of Mr Curtis moved away. Relief was sighed. Gretton smiled to himself. That was his kind of lead singer. That *was* his lead singer.

And anyway, it was time for the bands.

▶▶▶

All the outfits in town were playing that night; every bloody half-happening combo, taking part in a kind of new band competition for the benefit of a couple of London Indie labels; it was called the Stiff/Chiswick test. No one minded they came from the South. Stiff were funny and no one knew where Chiswick was.

And for Wilson, the night would answer a very special question. What made him so clever?

First, though, he had to cope with not being clever.

His and Razzer's band were given an early slot; a pre-launch try-out. The band had tried various lead singers. None had worked. Sacking the two who had actually rehearsed had already demonstrated to Wilson that this was no easy job. Playing with egos, ambitions, other people's dreams. Painful and highly unpleasant. By the time they had got to this night at Rafters, 'work' had truly commenced. Hearts had been broken.

So, no lead singer. The revolution meant not giving a fuck, so Wilson suggested to his group that they just do instrumentals. Why? Why fucking not? Particularly when the instrument is played by an angel.

But tonight the angel was singing. Fuck.

As good as this Vini kid was on his guitar, that crap was his singing. Wilson and Erasmus hadn't planned this. But in the punk spirit of 'do whatever the fuck you want', the band was doing just that. Fuck.

Wilson settled into the crowd and into the 'what the fuck' spirit that he was talking up when his internal monologue was disturbed by a voice to his left.

'You have to stop him singing, Tony.'

It was Ryan, local stringer for the London music press, for a music mag that had got stuck in time, like the tosser now taunting our hero.

'It's avant-garde, Ryan, you wouldn't understand.'

'It's very poor.'

'It's provocative.'

'Provocatively poor. Appallingly poor. They'll never call you the new George Epstein, you know.'

'That's Brian Epstein.'

'No, George Epstein.'

'It's Brian Epstein, you dick.'

'No, Brian Martin, the producer, George Epstein the manager.'

'George Martin was the fucking producer, you...'

'Tell him to fuck off,' chimed in an annoyed Erasmus, who was getting ready to push the twat over.

'Never be as important as Colonel Sanders and Elvis,' added the smug journalist.

That was the bad thing about the New Journalism. Cop a bit of Tom Wolfe or Hunter S. Thompson, get a bit of ellipsis down your grammatical throat and any fuckwit could sound cool and intelligent and actually did. Despite having the sense and sensibilities of a bucket of silage, any modern music journalist with a grasp of the new prose could hold his own as a knowing counter-culture hero and guardian of the gates of fame. Tossers.

Silence is, of course, the lesson. The press are frequently the most dizzyingly incompetent arseholes that God has put on this earth. The mistake is to reply to them. Wilson and Erasmus turned away from gnat-brain and got on to listening to what indeed was provocatively poor. But he didn't need this numb-nut to fucking tell him. He would sort it. They would sort it.

10
THE LAST BAND OF THE NIGHT

'The introduction doesn't normally go on this long. It's just that we're waiting for our singer. I think he's in the toilet.'

And Bernard Sumner leant back into his guitar and continued winding up those bar chords. It was late. Approaching two o' clock. The plugs would be pulled soon. The guitars and drums churned on. There was a throb about the chord progression. Something mighty going on even before Curtis began pushing his way through the crowd from the back of the room.

He jumped on stage, took the mike and a song called 'Digital' took off. Like a Saturn Five to which every fuckwit in the room was tied by a big piece of bungee chord. The guy in centre stage was at the centre of a storm. His own storm.

A chorus exploded, words stark and short, repeated over and over and over again.

Wilson had seen this kind of stuff once before – Van Morrison, late-sixties God, gone soft in the seventies.

You breathe in you breathe out you breathe in you breathe out...

He recognized again the miracle of afflatus; Dionysiac revelry, automatic voices, content pouring from the mouth and the soul. Unbidden, unstoppable.

And the answer was there, centre stage. Wilson the solipsistic academic had noticed with a little ego massage that he had got the bands right that he put on telly. Proud as he was of the debuts he had given the

Pistols, Clash et al, he privately revelled in the underside of this iceberg; the 200 other acts he hadn't given air-time to. And he'd got 100% in that exam too. That love of being right, the lower-middle-class lad from Salford's protective blanket of righteous rightness, had found a new oxygen. A&R. Picking bands. Picking art.

But he had wondered where the correct art-critical judgements were coming in from.

Now, finally, he understood the straightforward filter in his head. He had chosen artists who 'meant' it. More than meant it. Had no choice. The stuff was as if it was forcing itself up and out of their psyches whether they fucking liked it or not. 99.99% of bands are on stage 'cause they want to be in the music business, they want to be on *Top of the Pops*, they want to be rock and roll stars. The very few are on stage because they have absolutely no fucking choice. Whatever is demanding to be expressed pushes them forward. No choice. And that night Warsaw had no choice but to be up there on that stage playing this searing music.

▶▶|

And there were other elements to this enchanted evening. The rhythm section. Peter Hook, bass low-slung, notes played high on the fretboard, beginning the reinvention of bass melody. Steve Morris, nice lad from Macclesfield, with nice lad from Macc jumper, and the pounding beat that comes from a youth spent listening to rock and roll. Barney, arm insistently dragging up and down the face of his guitar, chords shimmering like brittle metal before returning to noise. F shapes, boys, F shapes.

And the lead singer. Later pinned to the specimen board as 'the dead fly dance', Curtis's movements were jerky, abrupt, an insane twitching response to what the music was doing to him.

Wilson had seen the future and Jon Landau could go and fuck off.

▶▶|

It was clearly time for Erasmus and Wilson to get in gear and get Vini and band on stage properly.

But 'provocatively poor'?

Of course. Provocation was fab.

Wilson sold his freebie Granada albums to pay the rent on a semi-derelict scout-hut in south Manchester. A rehearsal room. The womb from which comes all our musics.

And they got rid of the singing. For a time.

A guitar, some noises. Simplicity. Surely this was punk too. So out of place, so self-contained. Isn't that what punk meant?

If it's not what it should be, then it's what it should be.

And Wilson gave the band a name. The Durutti Column.

Buenaventura Durutti was a cool dude. A Spanish anarchist who led a team in the civil war against Franco, called the Durutti Column.

But that isn't where the name came from.

Keep up, keep up.

In 1966, a bunch of proto student revolutionaries, fired with the cult brand of anarchist theory that goes by the name situationism, took over the student's union at Strasbourg University, just by turning up for the elections. They spent their entire annual funding on creating a massive comic strip which they then flyposted overnight in their city. The Strasbourg morning rush hour was brought to a halt by a city-sized comic strip.

One of the panels featured two cowboys talking about reification. This panel was called 'The Return of the Durutti Column'.

So now you know.

On this occasion we're not going to suggest you read more. The legendary US rock critic, Greil Marcus – whose book *Mystery Train* is exhibit one in the case for rock 'n' roll being more important than oil painting – did *read more*. Sadly.

After approximately two years staring at the sticker of two cowboys talking French to each other that came with the first Durutti Column release, and which the poor Bay Area Dr Johnson stuck to his cassette deck, he decided to *read more*. He became the world's expert on situationist anarchism and was lost to the world of great rock writing until his 2000 meisterwerk on Clinton and Elvis.

Now *that* you should read.

11
REVERSING A TREND

The Durutti Column were ready.

Now, if you're breaking down the barriers with revolutionary music and a revolutionary name, then you can't possibly use an established club for the first full gig. New music means new time means new space.

Erasmus suggested the Russel Club, a West Indian night-spot in Hulme in inner-city Manchester. Like every other inner city in the West, it was as OUTER city as it gets. Outer sight, out of mind, outer fucking limits. Nothing bleeding inner about it.

The south side of Manchester had been settled by the Irish in the nineteenth century. Couple of square miles of little terraced houses that had become the North of England's definitive slums a hundred years later. Wilson's dad had been brought up in Hulme in days somewhere in between. His grandma, a theatrical, had worked the end of her life at the Hulme Hippodrome. Running the box office, perhaps. He was never taken to see Gran at work. It was a strip club. Entertainment city, this Manchester, England.

One step further south, across Moss Lane East, but let's say across 110th Street. This was Moss Side. It's where the *Windrush* ran aground. West Indian? Kingstown on the Medlock. Erasmus, while never playing the rasta card, knew just the right place for curried goat and peas. And Shorty's on the Front Line. Fried Chicken? Colonel Sanders, do one.

Wilson and Erasmus had been around. Some late teens in Manc played the Maileresque hipster by going to black clubs like the Nile and the Reno, and something that sounded like it was called the Edinburgh but obviously wasn't; all serious, get-down shibeens that lived on the Hulme-Moss Side marches.

And Erasmus had been checking the Russel, down in Hulme, where his dad used to take him.

We're not trying to get into the McLaren ten rules or do some Bill Drummond guide to the business, but if you want a piece of advice, this is it. An easy deal, folks. Want a club? Don't bleeding build one. (Did I say that – don't bleeding build a club? Oh, God, try and remember that for later – remind me when Gretton suggest building a club so he can ogle pretty girls, please.) Find some place that's doing shit business on a certain night and offer your good self as social secretary. They'll be happy to have someone rustling up punters and you've got a new home, a physical space that you can fill with your dreams and invite your friends to; your own Abbey Theatre, your own Algonquin.

In this case the Russel Club, Royce Road, Hulme.

The Russel was a big, black room, low ceiling rising over a rudimentary dance floor in the centre, and a fair-enough stage diagonally cutting the far corner; peeling wooden stools and tables, the bisexual perfume of stale beer and dope smoke. There was an upstairs, but you wouldn't know it.

'No Tams allowed' was the dominant motif throughout the club on half a dozen signs. What the fuck does that mean? If you have any friends who are Yardies, I suggest you ask them.

Erasmus and Wilson drove up through the new Hulme – didn't tell you they've pulled the slums down. Razed to the ground. And raised in their place, a monument to the acme of technological architecture: System Building.

Bastards.

You know, there are some lawyers and architects who are actually nice people. At home with the dog, probably. But at work? Fuck 'em.

Culpability must attach to stupidity. In this case the architects had good intentions. Aware that destroying the little terraced streets might destroy 'the community', they reinvented the little terraced streets. In the sky.

Deck access, guys. It was deck access. A series of monumental sweeping concrete curves, six storeys high, half a mile along. And the decks, the fucking decks. These were not community streets – these were concrete run-off channels for stale piss.

And when the developers were going for the gig, you know what the pitch was? A model of the Bath Crescents. Georgian Nirvana. Fucking cheek.

As Erasmus and Wilson drove the pale blue Mark One Escort RS 2000 under the shadow of Charles Barry Crescent, Hulme was going through its mid-life crisis. Having re-slummed the entire south side of the city, the nice families had moved out and it was problem family time. Good idea, that. That's why they call them the Projects; it's some dickwit's pet project. Ooh, problem estate; let's put problem people in them.

Stairwells. That's the phrase. Stairwells. Pissed in and lurked in. Yeah, rich man, have your nice house, but just walk this way home. Please.

A couple of years later, Hulme entered its glorious and glamorous old age when the problem families moved out. Replaced by drug dealers, musicians, astrologists, videomakers, and students who couldn't find their way back to mummy. Hulme was fantastically cool for a while before they pulled it down again. But not that afternoon.

'Are you sure the car will be safe, Al?'

'No problem, Tony, stop worrying.'

'It's a bit grim,' said Lindsay.

'Yeah, grim, industrial, that's good,' said Wilson, peering back a second and then a third time at his car.

The front door was open. They walked straight in. At the bar, cashing up, a tall, striking, late-middle-aged man in a fine cashmere overcoat. Imposing wasn't the word. Self-assured as only someone who took on the Krays and lived can be. Story was, he came from the tenements of Dublin's North Side, tough as those streets. After a slight altercation with London's premier crime family, he had come north.

'This is Mr Tonay.'

'Hi.'

'And this is Tony.'

Wilson set off on a ramble about New Wave music and the people of Manchester needing a place to express themselves.

'To get in a club these days you have look like a hairdresser,' said Lindsay.

'My wife's a hairdresser,' said Tonay. Another short circuit to the conversation.

Alan tried to get a little leverage.

'Tony's on television, Don. Sorry To, Don doesn't care much for TV.'

'Know what I call it, I call it the Idiot Box,' Tonay smiled. Threateningly.

Wilson took this with some ease; he thought people who didn't like TV were cool. And we know about insults and ducks' backs and Wilson's back.

'Yeah, you take the door, I take the bar. You can have Fridays.'

It had not been a cultural discussion. But it was done. But no, it seems Wilson has a problem.

He ushered Alan and Lindsay towards the stage area as Don continued to cash up.

He was deeply concerned about the lines of command. 'We have a problem.'

'What's that?'

'Well, he's called Tony and I'm called Tony.'

'No, he's called Tonay, Don Tonay.'

'Well, there you go, he's Mr Tony and he's Don Tony and I'm just plain Tony. This won't do.'

'Not Tony, for fuck's sake,' said Alan, whose Zen patience was crumbling. 'TonAy, alright, TonAY... anyway, you can call him Don and you can be Tony. It'll work.'

Wilson gave this his careful consideration.

'Alright, it's liveable with.'

▶▶▌

They left the club together, Don walking towards a Transit van driven by a striking-looking lady who might have done things for money.

'What kind of music are you going to put on?'

'Oh, post-punk, New Wave, Indie.'

'Indian? None of that shite, fucking ska music.' And he spat.

'Nice car, Don,' said Wilson, by now grovelling to the main man.

'One word of advice, get some heavy metal on, those fuckers drink like the Queen Mother. See yer later.'

'See yer, Don.'

Our team settled into the Wilson Escort.

'I could have been a Don,' said wistful Wilson.

'I could have been a Virgil,' said Erasmus, 'but my mother lost her nerve.'

'No, he means a don at Cambridge, Alan.'

(Actually he had got a shitty 2.2 which distressed him to the end of time, and he couldn't have made don, but he had had dreams.)

'What shall we call the club?'

'Let's call it the Factory,' said Alan.

'Excellent, very New York.'

'Very L.S. Lowry,' said Lindsay.

'No, I just saw a sign saying "Factory Closing". I thought we could put up a sign saying "Factory Opening" and reverse the trend.'

12
THE COLLECTED WORKS OF JAN TSCHICHOLD TURN UP

Opening night was just cool; a fair crowd, though not to see the extravagantly titled Durutti Column. Alan and Tony had invited some mates to play on these first Friday nights. Here was Margox and the Zinc, a female Adam and the Ants from Liverpool; Cabaret Voltaire, synth terrorists from Sheffield. And Rob's band, Warsaw, or whatever they were calling themselves.

What a night.

Erasmus and Wilson had had a big yellow-and-black sign made up at one of those places that make cheap 'Sale – everything must go' signs in dayglo.

It said 'The Factory' and went up on the side of the building.

And Wilson commissioned a great poster from a great young graphic designer.

A few months earlier Wilson had been at a bad Patti Smith gig. When it was New York poetess playing at being a rock star (and John Cale was floating her vocals in the dead centre of your head) it was art – when it was rock star playing New York poetess, then it was shite.

And this was a shite night.

But for a chance encounter.

'Excuse me, Mr Wilson, I'd like to introduce myself, I'm studying typography at Manchester Poly, I know who you are and that you do lots of things and if you ever need any graphics, I think you should use me.'

A phone number was given or taken. A connection made.

Thank God for Patti Smith. It wasn't just *Horses* that changed Wilson's life.

It was two months later that Peter Saville, a sort of twenty-year-old Bryan Ferry look-alike with searingly intelligent eyes, turned up at the Granada canteen to see Wilson.

Over a cup of GTV coffee, Peter showed Wilson a book on Jan Tschichold. He showed him the Penguin Crime covers from 1941, the constructivist play posters from the 1920s and the cover of the 1965 Hoffmann-Laroche catalogue (the Swiss chemical boys who did so much for the neural pathways of the second half of the century in question).

Wilson was entranced. Another fucking genius. The utter commitment of this kid said soul brother.

Do a poster for the new club we're doing. Scribbling down the details. Names, dates.

This wasn't Peter's first job. He told Wilson he'd done a promotional leaflet for a local mixing desk firm. The boss had been a co-hipster with Wilson a few years back in the trips down the Reno. Wilson ran into him.

'Hey. I'm using the kid you used, Peter Saville.'

'Yeah, he's great.'

'What's he doing for you now?'

'What?'

'What's he doing for you now?'

'Nothing.'

'Why? I thought you said he was great.'

'He's great but he's useless. The brochure turned up three weeks after the exhibition we needed it for. Great brochure, though.'

▶▶▌

And now it's opening night and the crowd is here just from word of mouth. Because there are no fucking posters up...

Two trips to Peter's sedate flat in Manc suburb Altrincham (upper-middle without much middle) to watch him arrange and rearrange black rectangles of thick paper on a big piece of yellow card did not elicit a poster for Erasmus and Wilson's venture. Zero.

'Do you mind if I go to the toilet?' said Scouse chanteuse Margox in the 8 feet by 10 feet dressing room that was squeezed behind the stage and which further squeezed the contained bodies of that night's musicians.

'Not at all,' said Ian Curtis and Steve Morris, a little dazed at such a personal question. Well, they were from Macc.

And Margox hitched up her skirt and sat in the tiny triangle that was the sink. Bidet-esque. White faces. Shock. Sound of running liquid. Wilson retreated back from the door, just in time to see Saville striding through the throng, with a big cardboard tube under his arm and mane full-on flowing.

'Jesus, Peter, what's that?'

'It's the poster.'

'But this is the gig.'

'So.'

Reasonable answer, thought the rapidly calming Wilson. Peter's aura of 'the artist' had that effect.

The yellow-and-black constructivist masterpiece was unsheathed.

'What's the point in bringing the poster now? This is the gig,' said Wilson.

'I know. I couldn't get the right yellow. Look, it does look brilliant.'

'It looks great but – it's too late.' Regret had now replaced anger.

'I know, I know it's late, but what d'you think?'

'It's absolutely bloody fantastic, but it's also useless. Nothing useless is truly beautiful, as William Morris once said... how many did we do?'

It was just so good. Yellow and black; a use of a thirties aesthetic that was to catch on about nine months later, but rarely done as well in Paris or on Madison Avenue. And this was for the fucking Russel Club in Hulme. Genius gets forgiven damn easily.

'How many did we do?'

'Three hundred.'

'Put them up. They'll be a souvenir of this great night. No, they'll be a memorial to an historic gig.'

'Now you see, they're beautiful.'

Peter has art that is never on time. Which is strange for a man whose early career consisted of inventing the 'Aesthetic of Appropriation', using pieces of the past that were exactly on time, fashionably early; on the zeit-geist, on the button, the only bits of the past that would make sense of today and tomorrow. But the artwork delivery process, it will never be on time. As many times as this story is written, his work will be late. He will not have done the cover of this book. Because if he had you wouldn't be reading it, because it wouldn't have got to the printers yet.

Peter says it's the difference between commercial design and problem-solving design.

Peter's mother said it was the entire change of blood when he was eight days old in the maternity hospital. Believe the mum.

Vini was OK that night, much better than at Rafters, but Hooky was better still. As Warsaw took the roof off The Factory, there was the odd Manc giving it a bit. After all this is the town where, five seconds into the one-minute meditation demanded by Mahavishnu John McLaughlin at the start of his classic 1972 set, a member of the audience suggested, loudly, that he 'Get on with it, you cunt.'

And who called Dylan 'Judas'? Yeah, that's us.

And this wanker at the front right as you watched the stage was giving Curtis some stick. It's a wonderful thing to see a musician coming off stage, face forward, bass guitar no longer slung just under his dick but now raised high in the air like a Mega Mohican tomahawk. Attttttaccckkkkk. Axeman. Yes.

And Hooky got back on stage after that one and the roof continued to rise. All the way to post-punk heaven.

Lindsay and Wilson gave Warsaw a lift home, only they weren't Warsaw any more. The car wasn't an Escort RS either. Reality check: four musicians, their manager, big manager, and a couple in the front. Naw. This was a 1974 Peugeot 506 estate. Classic bastard, maroon, three rows of fucking seats. Commitment to art. Boy racer collector's item traded in to some dodgy bloke in Brixton and this musician-carrier found, begging to be put to use, delivering tunes, in a garage forecourt in the Peak District. It signalled intent. As did the band now sitting in said maroon hearse.

'We've got a new name.'

'Why?'

'You can't put Warsaw on a poster. Everyone would think it was a holi-day advert.'

'Joy Division. Do you know what that is?' asked Ian.

'I think so. When the Germans used to pick out women they thought were racially pure and make them have sex with them.'

'Bit Nazi,' mused Wilson, the former International Socialist. (One week only; Fulham and Kensington Branch, 1971, tossers.)

'Yeah but it's also kinda cheery,' said Barney. 'You know, JOY.'

Rob had a half-smile. Let it happen. His way. Forcefully quiet, our Rob. This would cause trouble but it would be his new buddy in the front seat who'd get the shit.

He could see the headline: 'Granada Man owns Nazi Nightclub'.

Wilson was easy. After all, it was still punk. Jordan's armband; Sid and the swastika doll on the sleeve art of that late-period Pistol's single. And since the music industry was an obscene form of prostitution, he was quite up for it. Wilson was easy.

Rod for his back. Absolutely.

And that front-page headline did happen, in *The Jewish Telegraph*. What the fuck?

13
ENTER THE DRAGON

We're on the Moors again. Our fair city of Manchester sits at the centre of a semicircular sweep of millstone grit. It's where sunrise happens out to the west, always there, your own personal horizon. Dark grey, very dark grey from where the city looks.

It's on the way to midnight, a car park on the tops between Burnley and Manchester. Two men wait in their Ford Capri. They're techies and they're building a company in a Domesday-listed shed in a little village called Worsthorne outside Burnley up in north-east Lancashire. They call themselves AMS. They're waiting. For the man? The hero of the hour. A battered unwashed tank of a Volvo estate pulls in and parks up. Martin Hannett gets out.

Enter the Nutty Professor of our tale, our very own Gandalf of the Poppy. Martin is a music fiend, and ex-bass player for Greasy Bear, Manchester's answer to the Grateful Dead. (The answer was wrong.) He has a degree in chemical engineering. This stands him in good stead when it comes to making high-grade sulphate in his bath, or when he starts hustling his way into recording studios giving it the technical talk. Large intake of drugs has left a continuously unbalanced smile in his eyes. But it looks like the brain that lies behind is well-honed.

Slim build, shaggy hair, handsome face under it all. He gets in the cramped back seat of the Capri.

This is their third meeting. The guys are working on cutting-edge digital technology, trying to build an echo machine that works not with tapes or great metal sheets, but with 0's and 1's. They have changed the sounds into bytes but need to know where the bytes go. Hannett had offered input through a mutual techie mate. Martin starts to tell the guys in the front seats about the sounds he has been imagining recently.

'I imagine what sound would be like if it had to travel through a completely different atmosphere, through strange weather and weird gravity. What would it be like? I thought it might be interesting.'

He was, of course, stoned out of his extremely large brain.

'I want to hear the sound of the moon moving round the earth.'

And so on. Strangely, the men take it all in. They too love sound. Somehow they understand the aural hallucinations that Hannett regurgitates.

It's midnight. They say thank you. They drive back down the mountain to their shed and get busy with the motherboard. Hannett drives down the other side of the moors to his motherlode. What drugs? Every fucking drug.

14
THE RETURN OF THE DURUTTI COLUMN

It's time to move the Durutti Column forward. The first three gigs have gone OK. A couple of tracks have even been recorded in a cheap local studio.

The fact that there's no band is not a problem. The side musicians all fucked off to play back-up to some kid with ginger hair and a penchant for soul and walking sticks.

And Vini is temporarily indisposed. He's been in bed for three weeks and has his door locked. He is later diagnosed as undiagnosable. Basically a tormented soul. Or well fucked up. Same thing.

But this is no problem. Alan and Tony have two tracks, and a great name, the Durutti Column. Well, Tony thinks it's a great name. There is a gentleness about Alan that just lets Wilson get on with his stuff. Nice of him, really. And anyway the pick-up band for the ginger one are calling themselves The Mothmen, so really no contest.

It was time to put a record out. Maybe on Eric's Records in Liverpool. The legendary Roger Eagle, DJ, reggae collector to God, guru to a generation and owner of legendary Scouse nouvelle vague venue, Eric's, is restarting his label and has rung Wilson to ask him to come in as A&R.

They plan to do a sampler, two bands each from Liverpool and Manchester.

Wilson drives to Liverpool to sort it out.

In a basement under Matthew Street they get down to it. OK, says Roger and his mate Pete Fulwell, eight tracks on a 12-inch, four bands, you bringing the Durutti Column and that mate of yours Rob Gretton's band.

'There's a problem here. I took some acid last night.'

'Shit, flashbacks?' said the Eric's boys.

'No, not that kind of problem; I was pretty out of it, sitting on a mate's floor rummaging his record collection looking for the scratches you get from that Rolling Stones sleeve, and I picked up a copy of *Abraxas* bought in Singapore. Did you know that they don't use cardboard in the Far East? They colour-print on thin tissue-like stuff and then double seal it in transparent plastic.'

Roger and Pete were listening. But didn't really know why. They now felt they had been correct about the flashback problem.

'It was just wonderful. Sensational in the full meaning of the word.'

'And?'

'And I think we can do a double 7-inch in plastic-coated tissue paper.'

'We want to do a 12-inch.'

'No, a double 7.'

'No, 12.'

'No, double 7.'

And on and on and on.

And back went Wilson down the M62.

'Alan, let's put the record out ourselves.'

'OK.'

15
ALL OUR BANDS
HAVE THE FREEDOM...

Joy Division were the secret to this particular release. They were getting talked about. Some guys from Warner Brothers sniffing around. But it was too early for the A&R bidding war. And anyway, Barney and Rob and Steve and Pete and Ian and Tony and Alan, they were all mates.

The meeting was in a pub out Macclesfield way. Drinks were bought, stools set up in a corner of the bar.

'We'd like to put some of your music out, lads,' said Alan. 'And I've been doing a bit of reading about contract law. I think we could offer–'

Wilson swept in front of Alan, took the baton without noticing that some other fucker had been carrying it and swept on to the head of the pool table.

'There's not going to be a contract. It's not going to be a company. It's going to be an experiment in human nature. In trust and idealism and principle.'

'I don't know. We've had some interest from the majors.'

'We are a major. Mentally, we're more major than anything.'

Alan is showing Bernard his latest signing. 'It's called Red Leb. From the Lebanon. Red and soft, feel.'

Ian is interested in the other deal.

'What's it called then, this record company?'

'Factory.'

'I like Factory. It's a little Andy Warhol.'

And a little bit Bradley Hardacre, the diligent reader might well add, with a cynical aftertaste.

Wilson perched, half-cross-legged, on a bar stool, holding court like the caterpillar on the mushroom: 'It'll be a co-operative. We'll pay for stuff, take the money and split the profits fifty-fifty.'

All this altruism was all very well, but this cunt did have a relatively well-paid day job. Idealism came easy to the armchair anarchist. Erasmus, who could have done with a bloody wage, assented in the corner, though God knows why. It sounded exciting, I suppose. It *was* fucking exciting.

'Couldn't we have one contract, saying there is no contract,' suggested Rob with unerring prescience.

'OK. You can have it signed in my blood right now. Got any paper? Got a knife? I mean it.'

Bravado has its own adrenalin. Gretton stepped forward with a smile and a mountain-climbing tool with an extremely sharp blade as part of its arsenal. Stepped forward a bit sharpish, actually. Wilson made a slight cut on the ball of his second left finger. The no-contract contract was then inscribed on the back of a mass-catering white napkin.

The musicians own everything, the company owns nothing.
All our bands have the freedom to fuck off.

Rob wanted to check it, carefully.

'I don't know. It's a bit messy, that signature. Will it stand up in court, d'you think?'

'You've had my blood, what the hell more do you want?'

'Well, what else do we get?'

'You get me and Alan, and Peter to design your sleeves... and we bring you the only man who should produce you.'

▶▶|

'Martin, are you recording the wind?'

Wilson had parked the Peugeot in the lay-by and walked up the sheep track to near a moorland ridge. Hannett, thickly wrapped against the autumn winds, was on top of the ridge holding a mike stick and microphone out at just above waist level.

'Not now I'm not. I'm recording Tony Wilson talking into the wind.' An annoyed young man.

'Sorry. I just wanted to see about you producing a record for us.'

'Who's us?'

'Factory, Factory Records.'

'What's my royalty rate?'

'No royalties, you get profits. We make you an equal partner. There's me and Erasmus and Saville, the kid who designed the Factory poster. And then there'd be you.'

'I only mix on 24-track; that's £50 an hour.'

Wilson paused long enough to work out four tracks, two hours each, £400, just doable: 'OK.'

'OK, see yer.' And he pointed his face and his microphone to the heavens.

16
FASTER BUT SLOWER

'Stop, stop that horrible, horrible drumming.'

Martin sits in the centre of his world. The chair at the centre of the great Strawberry studio mixing desk. Thirty-six tracks, the dog's bollocks. If there is a power chair in life it is the producer's seat when art is happening behind the thick glass screen. The musicians stand and sprawl and play. The Man is at the controls.

Playing at the moment is Steve Morris, drummer for Joy Division.

'What's wrong with my drumming?'

'It's not your drumming as such, it's the nature and history of percussion. People have been drumming for twenty thousand years and they're not getting any better at it. Let's stop, let's reinvent the whole notion of drums.'

Steve hits the kit a few more times. It's like being at fucking school.

Hannett hits the studio talkback button again.

'There's a rattle...'

Hooky, not only nascent Viking bass god but also a great guy to have around if your car breaks down, offers some help.

'Maybe we could...'

'What? What do you know? What do you want?' This was Martin's ship. Does a deckhand discuss navigational issues?

'I was thinking. You know the high-hat...'

Hooky hasn't given up.

Martin completely ignores him.

'There's a rattle. You'll have to disassemble the entire kit. Every screw, every strut, every spring. Take it all apart and then reassemble it.'

It is a measure of the Merlin-like mantle that Hannett had already at this early stage created for himself that the poor fuckers started doing it. And continued doing it.

Wilson is at the back of the studio, having just brought Gretton a cup of tea. And a sandwich. White bread and no fucking green stuff.

'Er, will this take a long time, Martin?'

Hannett swivels to face Wilson. Stares. Silence.

'Is it still £50 an hour?' Wilson enquired timorously, as the group got to work with screwdrivers and pliers.

'We're working, aren't we,' dismissed Hannett.

Another bit of withering. Reply enough. Wilson goes back out to the pool room. What the hell is happening? Fifty pounds an hour. Jeeeeeesus.

And the reader is probably also asking the *funding* question at this point. Particularly as Steve's drum kit was not fully reassembled until 4.30pm the next day. Well, it's like this.

Wilson's beloved mother had died mercifully suddenly in 1975, leaving her beloved son £12,000 in Nat West Unit Trusts. He had figured £5,000 would get this record company thing up and going. Martin, however, was up and going for the £12,000 and by the time the art was captured, the Nat West Unit Trust scheme had lost one petty gambler.

And things got weirder that second night, with Steve Morris back in the drum booth.

Martin was fussing with a bunch of DI wires. He was busy installing a little black box on the side of the mixing desk.

'What's that gizmo, Martin?' asked Hooky.

'It's called Digital. It's heaven-sent.'

Yes, the two techies from the other side of the Moors had done their magic; this was it, the first binary echo machine in the known world. A Digital Delay.

And the engineer was busy in the loo. A small cubicle toilet in the Strawberry basement had been commandeered. An Aurafone speaker set up on the lavatory seat, and a stand mike about 18 inches away pointing at said Aurafone. Upstairs the feed from the drum booth was rooted to the toilet and then the input from the mike was put back in through the cool new piece of AMS outboard. Martin was removing all the nuances of sound that a real room could create in the human ear, and then adding the reverb and delay of his own imaginary room, his special world of sound that would change the ways drums sound for ever.

Boom. Boom. Steal me.

17
SHOT BY BOTH SIDES

The Factory club was taking its toll on the spirits of Erasmus and Wilson. Break even or loss, counted out in £5 notes on the barrels in the store room of Don's club. An empty venue chilled the soul of these two who took it personally and in the wallet.

And then it took its toll in other ways too.

The threesome of Lindsay, Razzer and Wilson were sitting on the low stools about fifteen feet from the entrance. They'd paid £300 to get this guerilla funk outfit called the Pop Group up from London. Presales stood at £35.00 and the fucking place was still empty at 9.30pm.

Suddenly, Alan pulled at Wilson's sleeve. And gestured towards the door. Wilson looked over and saw one of the most beautiful sights a man can see. Forget the *Water Lilies* or the Vatican Pieta. This was a queue. A bloody queue. Wilson smiled a deep, lingering, pleased smile.

Lindsay had missed the sleeve-pulling and only looked round to find her husband obviously silently greeting some girl coming through the Russel front door.

That was it. Two nights ago she'd watched in horror as, on his local TV 'What's On' round-up he had introduced, gushingly, this Debbie girl from New York. Although the green slime stuff that her guitarist Chris Stein had plastered all over the top of his guitar neck was fairly impressive, and the version of 'X Offender' was pretty raucous, the moment that mattered was when Blondie took the single-stemmed rose that she'd been fingering and handed it over to the beaming guy in the man-from-C&A suit. Bad move. Lindsay immediately assumed that something was going on. She was pissed off. More than normal, which is more than enough.

And now some slut in the club as well. Lindsay got up and walked away. She headed straight for the far side of the club where she'd seen Devoto. Our Howard, who had started the whole show rolling with the Pistols gig, had split from Buzzcocks and was now going his way with an avant-garde pop thing called Magazine. The mekon looks had been honed into charismatic semi-stardom. That night was the first step that led Lindsay and Howard to a hotel room in Leeds, and led Lindsay and Tony into a serious bout of revenge fucking.

'How was it for you?'

There is a story – completely untrue – that she fucked Howard Devoto in the Russel Club toilet that night because she'd caught our hero with a couple of prostitutes in the back of Don Tonay's van. It's worth recounting for the observation that it was all taken out of proportion.

'That was just a blow job. This is full penetration. Where are the car keys?'

And whatever it was, it was out of all proportion. And Wilson didn't notice a single thing, even when she snuggled up to Howard on other side of the dance floor. He was still looking at the door.

'Fucking hell, a queue. Fucking great.'

18
TO THE CENTRE
OF THE CITY

Martin is sitting at the mixing desk, staring straight ahead. Pupils ulti-mately contracted. What drugs? Lotsa drugs.

The mix ends.

Martin, startled, jumps up from the producer's chair.

'What's that? What's that gold shiny thing? It's not a halo, is it? I'm not dead. Am I dead?'

'No, Martin,' says Ian. 'It's a gold disc. 10CC, "I'm Not in Love".'

'I'm not in 10CC, am I?'

'No, Martin, you're in Stockport.'

It was a great mix.

The group piled into the Peugeot hearse to take a listen. Serve chilled and listen while driving.

Listening is intense until Ian says quietly and a little resentfully, 'I sound like Bowie.'

'That's alright, you like Bowie.'

'I hate Bowie. In "All the Young Dudes" he says you should die when you're twenty-five. D'you know how old he is? He's fucking thirty, well, twenty-nine. He's a liar.'

'A lot of artists do their best, transcendental, work in their late period when they're older. Think of Beethoven or Yeats.'

'Never heard of Yeats.'

'Yeats is one of the greatest poets since Dante, and if he'd died when he was twenty-five years old...'

'I'd have heard of him.'

The stunning musician's logic quietened the driver and full concentration was returned to the track.

Bernard offered an opinion. 'This is good.'

Rob, with that sense of how he knew it all the time, grinned. 'This is fucking special.'

'Special,' murmured the driver as the future came slowly into focus to the sound of the greatest rock band in the world.

For him and fuck the rest of you.

19
LOOKING FOR
A CERTAIN RATIO

Joy Division were part of their label, but they weren't Razzer and Wilson's band. They were Rob's band. Totally.

The boys decided they needed a band. In the Durutti Column they had a concept. They had a concept that had an album that had been recorded in a three-day session up in Rochdale. Vini had only turned up for the first day, but the ten guitar tracks he had played that day sat atop a bed of noise and triggered beats that triggered the soul.

But a band. Vini had not turned up for days two and three and had retired to a bedroom and a woman somewhere while the psychiatric staff at the local bin continued to investigate the uninvestigable; the relationship between Mr Reilly's stomach and his cerebral cortex. The relationship between genius and being fucked up.

So they wanted a band. And Rob gave them an idea. Sent them to look at a bunch of kids going by the name of A Certain Ratio. Love at first sight. The first five seconds had become central to the Wilson school of popular art criticism. This one took three. It was the look. Simple, second-hand demob suits. Grey cloth, white shirts. Trim, short hair. Thin. Intense. Three boys with guitars, grinding guitars and a mesmeric lead singer, Simon Topping, holding a noise box between his fingers and twisting a knob now and again, and twisting the audience now and again. The all night party just goes on.

It was the nearest a Manc band really got close to the Velvets, which after all is what every real band on earth wants to get close to. And the fact that these grinders of noise went out after rehearsals to dance at Pip's nightclub was the special twist required of great pop art.

Then came the addition of a funk drummer in the form of a Wythenshawe white man (he was the kind of black boy whose manners and standards are more white lower-middle-class English than Typhoo tea), Donald Johnson was his name. Described by a friend who I am happy to steal the epithet from as 'a poor man's Billy Cobham'. Donald's inclusion was a brilliant idea. At first. Funk and punk. Intoxicating. Wilson was in his element and Erasmus was back driving vans to airports late.

We need flight to feel the light...

Hypnotic fucking stuff, and a unique sense of style.

Arriving in London for a breakthrough gig at the London Lyceum, Simon had turned to his management team on arrival in the dressing room.

'Can you go to Lawrence Corner and pick up five sets of Sixth Army desert shorts and shirts?'

'Lawrence who?' asked Wilson.

'Lawrence Corner. You mean you don't know the best ex-army store in London?'

'No, Simon. I do not.'

'It's up by Euston on the road to Camden Town. Fucking hurry up.'

'It's useful to worship art. Because it makes it easier to be a complete fucking lapdog to any arrogant little twat who happens to make that art.'

Wilson headed up to said shop and purchased said gear.

And on the way back to the Aldwych he even picked up a spray can of fake tan. Going Ibiza ten years early.

Donald wasn't sure.

'We look like Hitler youth.'

'You don't, Donald, you're black.'

'Scouts; kinda scout look.'

'One slight problem,' said manager Wilson, 'your legs are reminding me to get chicken drumsticks for supper. Come on, let's get a bit of this tan stuff on 'em.'

And that night, with their Alamein looks and Simon and Martin adding rudimentary (yeah, punk) trumpets to their attack, they blew fellow pretenders Echo and the Bunnymen and Teardrop Explodes off the fucking stage.

Yeah?

Yeah.

And that was the high-water mark.

Donald had added precision funk drumming but had also let in the twin diseases of musicianship and ego. Suddenly they were moving towards jazz; all form and technique and no soul. And Donald's significant psychic presence was one of the reasons Simon, the main man, began to retreat. He retreated behind the trumpet and then behind the timbales and then behind a girl singer called Tilly. He just retreated till there was less even than the smile of a Lewis Carroll cat. Just a memory of the searing band that he had fronted.

Let's not blame Donald; something else may have influenced Simon in bailing out on stardom. He formed a relationship, a close one, with Ian Curtis. They were Factory's lead singers, playing at Factory nights across the country and across the channel. There was mutual respect, particularly from Simon for Ian. So what happened next may explain all. What happened next may just have done his fucking head in.

20
ANOTHER
PIECE TO CAM

After failing in a variety of daring stunts to get rid of me, Granada Reports *have asked me to go out on a skid pan. Great, throw some flash sports car around for an hour or so. No such luck. They want me to drive a bus on a skid pan. Do a few handbrake turns in a bus. Worse than that. A double-decker bus. Well here goes.*

On a wet morning in Ardwick the sight of a great yellow-and-red double-decker swinging and rolling on wet cobbles made good television.

How wouldn't it? Surely as the behemoth swung violently back on itself, tipping, tipping, leaning further and then crashing back onto its inside wheels, surely it must tip over sooner or later? The anticipation of the grinding of metal and sinew always makes for a must-see watch.

And here on that wet morning in Ardwick, Wilson was acting out one of the great adages of the music industry, the one that comes straight after 'never do a deal in Portugal'. And 'never sign a band with a backdrop'. This one was 'never give up your day job'. And Wilson hadn't.

The *Ripley's Believe It or Not* of local television magazine culture provided both a reasonable income on which to move freely in other areas while providing an ironic counterpart to those other areas.

And said areas were getting a bit serious.

Joy Division's first album, *Unknown Pleasures*, was a wildly reviewed cult hit. Factory had pressed 10,000 copies, and shipped 5,000 straight off to the new web of independent distributors and shops. The other 5,000 were brought back to Alan's Didsbury flat – its dark, first-floor, bay-windowed front room had become the *de facto* company offices. Wilson and Erasmus managed to be out the night the truck came north, and bass god Hooky had to carry the boxes up two flights of stairs. Yeah, a co-operative.

And Factory was getting a reputation, fuelled by the growing awareness of Rob's lot, other radical releases by the likes of A Certain Ratio, and Saville's utterly contemporary imaging; a process of grand theft of multi national logo precision and the flawless reappropriation of a variety of twentieth-century art movements. How to make a cottage industry coming out of Erasmus's Didsbury flat look different from every other fucking cottage in the world. Packaging that made the multi nationals look fucking cheap. Great idea. Except no one had the idea. They just did it 'cause they wanted to. Because delivering 'music' to the public was a religious activity, and these Catholic boys knew about packaging religion. The Sistine Chapel's been top PR for several centuries.

And the no-contract contract meant that Factory was by now picking up numerous waifs and strays who were making real music. Orchestral Manoeuvres had been about to give up and go back to work at the Post Office in Birkenhead when Lindsay had suggested to the man driving the car that he play that six-month-old cassette of a song called 'Electricity' on the car stereo again. And again. And again. The Distractions were power pop from very south Manchester, with an ace ditty called 'Time Goes by so Slow'. There was Section 25 from the cash economy seaside town of Blackpool, with their uniquely uplifting brand of melancholia; a reggae outfit from the local ghetto called Exodus; and a bunch of crusties from Tyneside, too early to be crusties, and just a bit too late for the avant-garde end of the English Civil War. They were called Crawling Chaos. Well, what do you expect from Geordies?

Fucking hell, Factory Records was a record company.

This was getting serious.

And it seemed to be getting a bit serious for Joy Division. The bit about meaning it was all well and good, but sometimes it felt like they meant it a little too much. Like Ian meant it a little too much. This impression was driven home the first few times Ian gave way on stage to his epilepsy.

Bands on stage. Our heroes rarely relate to each other, their postures, projection and eyelines being for you, the audience, alone. Bass players and drummers who incline heads and together wind the rhythm up are just a little bit bass-slappy embarrassing and hardly add to the spectacle.

But Joy Division presented a special *esprit de corps* on those nights it was required. Towards the end of a set, as 'Transmission' would rev up and Ian hit the third verse at top intensity straight out of the second chorus, Bernard and Peter would angle in and watch their lead singer carefully. They could see that the insane spastic movements of Ian's arms were getting a bit turbo, they could see that he was meaning it too much.

How long then? Some nights, to the end of the set, some nights, to the end of just that song. And Ian would scatter the mike stand, stagger speedily sideways and be rushed off the stage by Hooky or Barney or Terry their road manager.

Holding him down was tough. Terry was best at it.

'How are you feeling?'

'What?'

'You OK?' said Rob. The van was quiet. A little aftershocked.

'It's nothing, shut up,' replied Ian curtly.

'Looked like an...'

'I said shut it.'

'So you don't want me to talk?'

'No, I fucking don't.'

'Not even to tell you that we're going to tour America?'

'What?'

'Fucking great,' from the back seat.

'Great. Do we get to stay in five-star hotels?'

'No, you stay in whorehouses and I stay in five-star hotels.'

They all took the piss out of each other for a while. Full of it. Ian too.

21
THE STUFF OF LEGENDS – THE DERBY HALL RIOT

A new Joy Division album was recorded down in London at Brittannia Studios. Hannett was mightily at home in the technocave of Pink Floyd.

And somewhere around then they all played the Derby Hall in Bury.

A Factory night was planned in the civic theatre in this nice-enough working-class radial town about eight miles north of Manchester. The only problem was, Joy Division were headlining and Ian was still recovering.

From an overdose of sleeping tablets.

Did we mention that?

The overdose of sleeping tablets was largely overlooked at the time, rather as it has been here. Yes, Rob and his group and his new business partners (oh, yes, we left that bit out too – but just the same, it just sort of happened that Alan and Tony invited Rob in as the fifth and equal partner 'cause his staying with Factory had cemented the adventure and no one made a fuss, so we won't either) visited the hospital and took it in turns to do the mate-with-a-poorly-mate bit.

It's disgusting the way some people quote Joy Division lyrics to explain Joy Division things. But a novelisation is an intrinsically disgusting art form and it's fair to say that Ian's mates saw this ingestion of negative chemicals as merely the cry for help he had written about so recently in *Colony*.

A song lyric! That's how the band and the partners saw Ian's overdose.

And they were all there to help, weren't they.

And anyway, there was that other line in *New Dawn Fades* about how a loaded gun wasn't the answer. How it wouldn't set you free. Thanks Ian, you've figured it. Go tell Kurt.

But as the positive ethic of that line sinks in, Mr Curtis adds a twist to his own tale and after a brief and evil fucking pause suggests that this affirmation of life is in fact merely your opinion. The opinion of the listener.

Not his.

Cheeky, no, nasty. Fucking musicians.

So the Bury Hall was a problem. After three weeks in hospital, Ian was out but weak and convalescing. Maybe he could do three numbers.

'I've got an idea,' said Wilson. 'It's a Factory night, so let's do a medley. We can get Ratio down and Section 25 from Blackpool, and that new lot with arguably the worst name in rock and roll history, Crispy Ambulance. Everybody knows each other's stuff. We can do a few ACR songs with Hooky and then change drummers and then some 25 stuff and then Ian can come on and do a couple of pieces and then we shuffle again.'

'Sounds fucking stupid to me.'

'No, Rob, it'll be great. We're a family, we'll do a family show and it means Ian won't have to knock himself out.'

'Still sounds fucking stupid to me.'

'No, Rob it'll be great.'

God, Ian was shaky that night. A crowd of around 300 for the word-of-mouth wonders. *Unknown Pleasures* was continuing to sell. This radical development of punk was out there, on kids' record players, on late-night radio stations. It was out there busily creating an audience for Joy Division and there were 300 of the bastards there that night – for Joy Division.

And they got a pretty weird downbeat version of 'Love Will Tear Us Apart' plus a couple more strange and doomy iterations from the catalogue before Ian walked back off to the left of the stage. He was passed on the stage stairs by ACR's Simon Topping.

The audience was not pleased. Not pleased at all.

As Simon arrived at the mike, a belligerent-looking Buryite halfway to the back of the hall turned to his mate: 'Fucking hell, it's that fucking guy from A Certain Ratio. They were here last week and I didn't like the funk bastard then.'

He'd obviously been making good use of his thick glass pint pot, because it was empty, and he now made even better use. He flung it at the stage.

It sailed over Simon's right shoulder and smashed against the back wall. The musicians went still. Gretton went nuts. He was standing on a dais at the back where the mixing desk was. It took less than a second for Wythenshawe's finest to hurl himself into the throng. He probably screamed some Wythenshawe war cry as he dived in but it got lost in the translation.

On stage, Terry the road manager was staring into the abyss, into the melee where his boss was laying about him and being laid about at. Terry was rigid with the ultimate dilemma. If he went in, he'd get the shit kicked out of him. If he didn't, Rob would kick the shit and the piss and most of the blood cells out of him.

Decision obvious, he seized the mike stand and went in flailing.

This small riot went on for around thirty minutes. The Manc boys generally defending side stage and making attacks from the bar, the Bury boys making mostly frontal attacks. As usual at a good gig riot, the carefully hurled bottle was the Cruise missile of choice.

Section 25's bass player, a serious full-on Buddhist, tried to explain alternative strategies to Rob, but he wasn't having any of it. But at least he was able to pinion the arms of his fellow bass player from behind and hold him and his four empty beer bottles contained for a while.

'Hooky, violence is not the answer.'

'Let me fucking go.'

'Hooky, this is not the answer.'

'I'll fucking kill them.'

In the dressing room after the war was over and number two roadie Twinny – pure Salford and had given as good as he got – had been despatched to the local hospital with Lindsay, Wilson noted Ian wasn't around.

'He's up in the coffee bar upstairs. He's pretty upset.'

When Wilson found the forlorn Curtis, he was sitting alone on an uncomfortable cane-backed chair and had his head in his hands.

'It was my fault, it was my fault.'

'What do you mean? It wasn't your fault.'

'Course it was my fucking fault.'

Wilson searched, remembered and hoped.

'Ian, there was a Lou Reed gig at the Free Trade Hall a couple of years back. He wore dark glasses all the way through and stood ramrod still at the mike and after fifty minutes of ice-cold intimidation went off stage, didn't come back, and it all went off. Were you there?'

'Yeah, when they put all the lights on and they had to call the police.'

'Exactly.'

Thank God for the Velvet Underground; what would we ever have done without them?

'Was that a great gig, a great event?'

'What?'

'How do you remember it? Was it great?'

'I suppose it was.'

'It was, you know it was, and tonight was major, a full-on art event. You've given these fuckers something to tell their children about.'

You know what's weird about this fucking story? People do tell their children about it.

⏭

And some fuckers never give up.

'Tony Wilson, what do you say to the charge that you're fascist?'

Wilson had made a stab at comforting Ian and was now on his way out of the building to find Lindsay and the Peugeot, which still weren't back from the hospital. And that fuckwit of a journalist, Ryan, was on his case.

'A what?'

'Your band, Joy Division are named after a group of women who were captured by the SS for the purposes of breeding perfect Aryans. Isn't that sick?'

'Have you ever heard of situationism or post-modernism? Do you know nothing about the free play of signs and signifiers? Yes, we've got a band called Joy Division. We've also got a band called the Durutti Column. I'm sure you don't need me to point out the irony there.'

He brushed the prick off.

And headed across the half-empty hall where another local band had taken over for the end of the night. It was The Fall. Super-proles. Like Bury, they were North. And took it upon themselves to hate South. Anything south of them. Anything even half a mile south of them. Which was Factory. And Wilson.

Maybe it was the spirit of the occasion, or maybe the fact that Wilson's wife had had a chat with the Fall's lead singer Mark E. Smith the previous weekend in the Cyprus Tavern, a crap venue back in Manchester. She'd gone up to him and told him what his problem was.

'You know your problem, Mark? You're middle class.'

Good one, incendiary even. Poor Mark E had no answer that night, but seeing the goon off the telly in his Paul Smith double-breasted was all it took.

'There's that wanker Wilson a pocket music vampire, the slut in the suit.'

'Thank you, Mark.'

'Maggie Thatcher's favourite bastard baby. Yes, you Wilson, she loves you yeah yeah yeah.'

Have a finger, Mark.

22
WHAT THE WAVES
WERE ALWAYS SAYING

Ian arrives after a long walk at Lindsay and Tony's stone cottage on the moors.

> *Lindsay opens the door.*
> *'Is Tony in?'*
> *'No, he's at Granada, come in.'*
> *'No, it's OK.'*
> *'Come in. You've come miles.'*
> *'It's OK.'*
> *And Ian heads back down the hill.*

Was the response really so empty?

Everyone tried to help Ian. Tried to help Ian? To the band and the partners it meant giving him somewhere to stay and recover away from his troubled home life, where he seemed to be having more and more rows with Debbie, his wife and the mother of his just-born daughter Natalie. But how the fuck was anyone going to really try and help Ian?

He stayed at Bernard's for a week. And then at Rob's, and then he moved to the Wilson cottage in Charlesworth for a week.

All very well of Wilson to invite him in, but he was off every morning to the day job at Granada, and Lindsay, who was already finding the TV-turned-revolutionary art-entrepreneur a bit much, was doing the babysitting. The revenge-fuck carousel was still going round, but with a house guest efforts were made to keep the marital shit from upsetting Ian, who was also in marital shit.

There was another woman. And as the usual the other woman is of course, THE woman. Her name, Aneek, a girl from Belgium, a big music fan. She booked a club called the Plan K in Brussels, which had been Joy Division's first date abroad. Her business partner in promoting bands was one Michel Duval, a young Belgian boy who gave up a career in the diplomatic corps to set up the first of Factory's myriad international offshoots, Factory Benelux. Michel read an early draft of this piece of shit (LA industry term of affection) and as a friend was upset to be left out, and besides which he's now a music publisher and that's where all the money is. And this is where he fits in.

And his friend Aneek had become more than a friend to the lead singer of Joy Division.

Wilson's efforts to entertain his troubled guest consisted of putting a dozen bookmarks in a copy of the collected poems of W.B. Yeats and hoping he would find them interesting; the main romantic ones, you know, the ones with historic sweep and also that one about Joseph liking the way his finger smelled. And then into the Peugeot and off to work.

Lindsay and Ian drove each other a little mad that week. And by Saturday, an on-cue marital explosion set Wilson off back down the mountain, Ian sitting quietly beside him in the Peugeot.

'Fucking bitch, I can't even look after my poorly friend.'

Except that he'd left her to look after his poorly friend for the entire week, so fuck him.

And Ian was taken to his mum and dad's in north Manchester for the final week before the big trip to America.

And when the end came it was as a result of a kindness. Which was nice.

The band were due to leave for New York on Monday morning. On the Saturday, Rob took Ian out for a haircut. Anticipation. Good vibes.

Now when it came to Ian's German-ness it was more Goethe than Goth; a hankering for the serious-hearted romanticism that gushes like the Rhine. Ian's favourite filmmaker, obsessively so, was Werner Herzog, and on that Saturday night BBC2 were showing *Stroczcek* late. Sub-titles are all very well for the young avant-garde, but Ian decided it would be unfair to put his mum and dad through art-house movie endurance and thought he'd go back to the then-empty terraced house back in Macclesfield.

His wife Debbie turned up, and there was a row.

And a deep sadness.

And there was a movie; the last line of Herzog's masterpiece endures in Joy Division's personal mythology: 'There's a dead man in the cable car and the chicken's still dancing.'

And hadn't Jon Savage's review of *Unknown Pleasures* in *Sounds* set the tone with its Tarot reference to the house of the hanged man?

When Ian was discovered on the Sabbath, hanging from a nineteenth-century device used to dry washing, they say that there was a bottle of whisky on the table. They say that Iggy Pop's *The Idiot* was still spinning, aimlessly, pointlessly on the record deck. The stylus arm had fully retracted. Hadn't it just.

23
EVERYONE NEEDS A BOSWELL, NO ONE NEEDS A LYING C**T

That Sunday, Wilson was working at Granada in the *World In Action* editing suites on the third floor looking out on to the Granada croquet lawn; don't ask.

Shortly after three o'clock, the phone went at the back of the cutting room. Wilson picked up.

'Rob, I'm working, what the hell is it?' Bad mood, a degree testy.

Rob didn't respond, snap back, nothing. He was with nothing.

'Sorry, it's just that Ian's dead. He hanged himself. They found him this morning.'

Pause.

'Where are you?'

'At home, Chorlton.'

'Right.'

It is perhaps some credit to Wilson's sense of delicacy or even journalistic professionalism that he turned to his colleagues in the cutting room, explained he had a slight problem and would need to go out for an hour, and ran off down the corridor. Without another word. If it is strange to mention good taste on the part of our hero, that's because in a couple of paragraphs' time the process is reversed, so bear with us.

Shock and horror shared, arrangements, practical ones, made, Wilson emerged from Rob's onto the nice suburban Chorlton side-street. To find the Peugeot parked sideways in the middle of the street, passenger door wide open and engine still running. Just as he had left it an hour earlier. Strange how when something really matters nothing else really matters.

Ian had been taken to the Chapel of Rest in Macclesfield. Sunday night. Visiting time. Like a bloody hospital, only it's a corpse not a patient you have to be on time for.

Having lashed out at the scum who represent the music press, it's time to back-pedal a way here and bring in Paul Morley. Paul had started a fanzine, pre-punk, from his Stockport bedroom and had progressed to being *NME*'s man in the north. He wrote like an angel. And he wrote about Joy Division and Factory, with a touch that made the arrogance acceptable and the art palpable. He was not part of the family, but he was part of the family. A journalist can't be part of the family, but a great writer can. So.

And that afternoon, as the youth culture crowd began to filter the news of their own Hendrix, their own Kennedy, Morley rang Wilson to see if it could possibly be true. When someone connected dies, you become like a US spy satellite picking up on all those conversations between the connected. Death is fast, but rumour is a little slower. Can it be true? Can it be true? How many phone calls before someone is actually dead?

And Wilson, after confirming Ian's leaving, suggested that Morley accompany himself and Lindsay to the Chapel of Rest that night. Morley demurred.

'Not really my place.'

'It is, I'll pick you up at 8.00pm.'

When they arrived in the Macclesfield side-street, Morley refused to get out of the car. That was fine. He just had to be around.

'I'm not here as a journalist, Tony.'

'It's not for now, but one day you will write about it – one day you'll write it.'

'I don't think I can.'

'Sure, you feel like that now. But we'll see.'

Ghoulish. Man selling death. Preparing the myth, polishing it.

Wilson thought he was doing Ian right. Preparing for history, adding the emotion to the language skills of the best storyteller around.

But ghoulish is OK.

"Ian Curtis's death is the best thing that ever happened to me," says Tony Wilson' was how *The Face* magazine dealt with this over-calculating reaction to the death of Ian a few years later. They dealt with it in 48-point bold type in the centre of a page and put it in quotes. Wilson was shocked; he'd always wanted to be Malcolm McLaren and outrage people, but was actually too much of a has-been altar boy to really get down there like Malcolm. So he was shocked that he might have said such a dreadful thing. And a day later, when he heard the Curtis family were upset, he rang *The Face* to ask if he had said it.

'Yes. This is obviously a pretty heavy thing, so we triple-checked and it's there clear as a bell on the cassette.'

'OK, I'm sorry to have troubled you. Er – what tape? I don't remember a tape.'

'He taped the interview and has the tapes with him in Paris.'

'Ohhhhh, I'm sorry. I wonder, could I have a copy of the tape?'

'Certainly, it'll be a couple of weeks.'

A couple of weeks stretched to five years and three months, at which point the former editor of *The Face* told Wilson at a seminar on Safer Dancing that in fact there had been no tape and no recording, that it had been made up, and that she'd been commanded not to mention it to me until five years, the statute of limitation for libel, was up. Cheers.

So, taking Morley in the back of the Peugeot to the Chapel of Rest – conscious of historic duty, or man readying himself to sell death? Who the fuck knows.

Of course, if he were to be allowed to defend himself he might point the reader to a far finer work called *Nothing* by the aforementioned Paul Morley.

If you know what I'm talking about, fine; if you don't, it doesn't matter but you *should* read more.

24
THE CHAPEL OF REST

'I know this is a bad moment but, you know, life goes on and they're going to need a lead singer. I know all their songs off by heart already.'

The real ghoul time. Jury not out on this geezer with a Cure sticky-up haircut who accosted Wilson and Lindsay on the way into the chapel.

'Don't lose any time, do you?'

'It's me singing. I sing all their stuff on there. Just get time to listen to it, Tony, I want to help, you know.'

'Yeah, OK I'll listen to it, OK.'

The brush-off comes easier with repugnance. Inside the small building, they run into Razzer coming out of the door to the lying-in-state room.

'Al, y'alright?'

'Yeah, his mum and dad are in. Just got there in time.'

'What do you mean?' asked Wilson.

'Well, his mum and dad were outside, and I checked him and he's got this fancy white shirt on but they'd left it down on his neck and you could see these great big bloody rope marks all round it.'

'Jesus, what did you do?'

'Just pulled the collar up and covered them over, easy.'

'Jeesus.'

Inside was nothing. The bit that's left. But maybe there was a bit of something else because quite openly and loudly, Wilson said, 'You stupid bugger.' So he must have though he could hear, or something not nothing could hear. And don't read tragedy or *weltschmerz* into that line. 'You stupid bugger' was a co-worker's resigned anger, frustration and fond annoyance at the main man retiring early from the scene. It was entirely appropriate. An honest valediction.

My editor is getting a little tired of the frequency with which this piece quotes from the literary canon. But Wilson went to Cambridge, and his college was home to the founder of the English novel, and the man who invented the idea that it was time 'for something completely different'. Hurrah for Lawrence Sterne, and no, you don't bloody have to read *Tristram Shandy*, but when a death happens in his book, you get a black page. A whole page in black. A nice big square of black ink. The real attraction is getting a page closer to the end without having to spew out 350 words.

Or explain.

But there's a better way. Let the ink on the page be Ian's:

Walk away in silence
See the danger – always danger
Endless talking – life rebuilding
Don't walk away – face the danger

People like you find it easy
Always in tune – walking on air
They're hunting in packs
By the rivers, through the streets
It may happen soon
Then maybe you'll care
Walk away
Walk away from danger
Walk in silence
Don't walk away in silence
See the danger – always danger
Endless talking – life rebuilding
Don't walk away
Walk in silence

Don't turn away in silence.
Your confusion – my illusion
Worn like a mask of self-hate
Confronts and then dies
Corrupts and then dies
Don't walk away

People like you find it easy
Naked to see – walking on air
Hunting by the rivers
Through the streets, every corner
Abandoned too soon
Set down with due care
Don't walk away – in silence
Don't walk away

25
TO BE OR NOT TO BE

Why?

Are you asking why?

Why not? It's natural. No, no, not suicide, asking why someone topped themselves.

Bernard always thought it was the medication that Ian took for his epilepsy.

Rob never said what he thought.

For many years, Wilson thought it was altruistic suicide. Romantic altruistic suicide. He had gone out with a sociology student in his teens and had a nodding relationship with Durkheim. And it was a simple, romantic answer: he was hurting his wife, his daughter and his lover – what better way to help everybody than by removing himself?

Stupid bugger.

Fast forward ten years to 1990 and the fancy Factory office whose extreme cost and hubris will inform the later phases of this book, and lead to the second round of catastrophe. An early-morning emergency financial trauma board meeting, number 437 out of 548, and strangely Wilson is there early. Because he'd spent the night on the IKEA deep-leather couch.

'Cause there was another woman in Wilson's life. And, yes, she was THE woman.

And nobody knew, except Hooky who had explained to Wilson that you should 'never shit a shitter'.

And arriving early and on his own for that morning's meeting; Hooky.

'How's life, To?'

Portrait of the artist as a young whippersnapper.
Already taking himself too seriously, don't you think?

On the set of *So it Goes*, 1976.
Before the Pistols there was only the llama.

An absence of dress sense for all to see. Check the bloody scarf.

Wilson tries politely to get Jon the Postman off stage. Kevin Cummins hovers with camera.

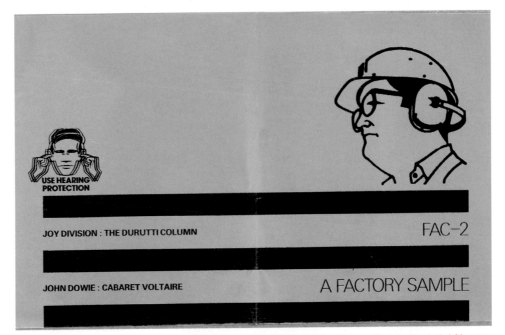

USE HEARING PROTECTION

JOY DIVISION : THE DURUTTI COLUMN

JOHN DOWIE : CABARET VOLTAIRE

FAC-2

A FACTORY SAMPLE

'This is the first release. We'll call it Fac 2 'cause it's a double single.' Of course.

The Durutti Column comic strip.

Early Factory Benelux flyer.

The Durutti Column: Vini Reilly and Bruce Mitchell.

Joy Division (Stephen, Ian, Bernard, Peter).

Ian Curtis.   Martin Hannett.

'Power, Corruption and Lies'. And a bowl of flowers by Fantin-Latour.

New Order (Stephen, Bernard, Peter, Gillian).

Two posters, from the Russel Club ('No, the first release isn't Fac 1, Fac 1 was my poster for the club' – Peter Saville invents numerology) to The Haçienda.

The Happy Mondays.

Excerpts from Fac 245, the
Factory Christmas Card, 1990.

It's not in the book, but these are Wilson's two wonderful kids, Olly the junglist and Izzy the spicy girl whose friends are becoming moshers. And it's not in the book, but Manchester United won the treble.

Announcing the closure of the Haçienda.

Yvette Dawn Livesey at the Trevi Fountain, 1992.

Anthony H. Wilson, 2001. Still standing.

'Fucking shit, Peter.'

'Now you know how Ian felt.'

'What?'

'Now you know how Ian felt.'

'How the hell did you know? I just figured it last week. I've spent the last seven days driving round in a dream; all I can think about is that this is why Ian did it. How did you know?'

'What d'you think happened to me, you dick?'

The Hook-Wilson theory is... but then, maybe it's private. Maybe you have to figure it out yourself, like Hook and Wilson. And if you don't keep reading, you never will. Which is a way to get you to the last page. So to hell with the theories.

Let's have the memories. To contradict the myth.

To talk about the japing, the ultra-professional personal trickery played by each member of Joy Division on the other; the rats released on to the Buzzcocks bus after the Apollo gig to say thank you for their ground-breaking support tour; the beds with the inside legs sawed half through to collapse in the darkest hours.

The 'jamming' of A Certain Ratio's Transit at 3.00am before the drive home to Manchester. Post-London gig and visiting with friends Joy Division at Britannia Row was followed by a trip back to the band's rented London flat in Marylebone. Coffees, beers, and for ACR and Wilson dope; Joy Division were never Class-B types. And then the goodbyes, the strange looks, the descent of three flights of stairs and out on the street, the first yelp of disgust and disbelief as the first grasp at the door handle of the van was uuuurcckky. Urrrrrrggggggghhh.

'What's wrong, Donald?'

'There's something horrible and sticky on the handle.'

'Any problems, guys...?' was the faraway question. From the high-up Georgian windows peeked the grinning heads of the darkest band on earth. And seconds later, from these windows, the eggs, the water and the flour. The northern-bound lot on the pavement had no choice – escape, run, grasp the jammy fucking handles before that... Arrrghhh.

The unpleasant manual discomfort lasted for the next four hours; all hands were sticky and just shitty. As dawn broke outside the Cheetham Hill lock-up rehearsal room, and hands went to get the gear. Urrggghhhh, fuck. 'Bastards.' Muttered, smiling.

Epilepsy, suicide and Wilson's favourite review line of all time: 'When Curtis sang "I hear them calling me", I promise you I could bloody hear them too. And hey, they were fun. Hear me, fun.'

Their visual biographer, a Manchester City fan with the most potent portraitist's art, Kevin Cummins, Morley's picture man and brother-in-arms, has in latter years taken to claiming the Curtis myth as his own creation: 'In fact, Ian was great to get pissed with, but has this image of a depressed reclusive gloomy romantic hero because I only released photographs of Ian looking depressed.' There you are. It's all myth and Kevin might as well have one of his own.

And two of the faces that grinned from the Georgian window frames in the early hours were Ian and Aneek.

And now the real memories invade.

Some weeks before Ian's departure, Wilson had to take the early-morning train to London for the day job. He'd had a temporary promotion to Britain's top current-affairs programme *World in Action* and had been summoned to a London meeting. Driving to Piccadilly station for the 7.30am he came up Ducie Street to get to the station car park when he saw, walking funereally, the lovers, Ian and Aneek.

They walked like they'd been walking all night.

They walked like they were in hell.

They walked like they were in heaven.

Wilson pulled over. 'Hello, you two; what are you doing?'

'Just walking. Aneek's got to get the train back to London.'

The answer was delivered slowly, resignedly, emptily. They had been walking the streets all night. Love with no place to go.

'Er, OK, see you on the train.'

Walking the streets at night and death are excellent bedfellows. Half of the titled cast list of Dickens's *Dombey and Son* die halfway into the book. Young Paul, the son of the title, is sickly from page one. Down at the seaside for his health, he keeps asking people what the waves are saying. The chapter in which Paul dies is called 'What the waves were always saying', and it's a chapter that Dickens wrote after walking the streets of Paris through a series of dark, long nights until the dawn. You walk the streets when you have nowhere to go, no home, no bed; you're lost. Death feels closer. That was how that early morning felt before the normalcy of the Pullman jerking out of Manchester Piccadilly for London Euston.

It is one of the many oddnesses of Macclesfield that this little piece of industrial town on the edge of Cheshire stockbroker belt, and just four miles from the village whose off-licence sells more champagne per annum than any other offie in the UK, this town famous merely for its worms having pioneered silk production in the textile-crazy North-West of England, this odd hybrid of a town has a station that every other London train stops at. It's like someone knew that Macc has a place on the world stage.

Wilson knew that the fifteen minutes to Macc would be Ian and Aneek's final moments for a while and left them to it.

He saw Ian on the platform at Macc, waving goodbye to Aneek. The grey raincoat, all-night exhaustion written on his face; or maybe the exhaustion at the emotions he was bombarded with, the ones he could or couldn't filter into his words, into his group.

After a polite ten-minute interregnum, Wilson made his way back to where Aneek was sitting in second class.

Idle chit-chat with a sad-eyed lady. Until mention of the new album brought it out.

'What do you think of the album then, Aneek?'

'I think it's terrible.'

'The album?'

'No, no, not the music, but what it is, don't you understand? He means these things, they're not just lyrics, they're not just songs, he means it.'

'Means what?'

'When he says, "I take the blame", don't you understand? He does exactly that, he thinks everything is his fault, it's just all too real.'

Wilson nodded. And thought nothing. She was in love, she took the music too seriously. She was Belgian, she took everything too seriously. It was just an LP. A great LP but not real, not life.

Wrong.

Totally fucking wrong.

INTERMISSION

26
WHAT THEN?

And that should be it. The end. Give up. Go home.

I suppose that's where the oral tradition comes in so neatly. Some guy's telling you this story – hell, it could end in the next minute or it could end sometime next month. There is the unknown, the possibilities.

But with this Gutenberg thing, you know there's still loads to go, because your right hand is fingering at least as many pages as it has taken you to find out what happened to Ian Curtis.

So you know it's not the end.

But it should have been.

You've got this record company thing, built on wilfulness, and an anarchic sentimentalism about the role of popular art. And it's all going great. And then you lose your lead singer. You lose your number-one asset. The main man. The Thing.

They should have given up, surely. Surely.

They should, and looking back on it it's a wonder they didn't.

But they didn't.

There were records to bring out. Ian's records. It was some time into Tuesday night when someone remembered that the soon-to-come *Closer* album sleeve by Peter featured a 'statue' of a woman grieving over a grave.

The artwork had been two months late, but that wasn't late enough.

'Oh, fucking hell.'

'It's too late, it's printed, it's done.'

And later it would be easy to claim that the death and attendant hoo-hah had sold the single and the album. Bollocks.

On the Friday previous, thirty-six hours and counting to lift-off, the sales rep for Island Records, the enthusiastic local music hustler, Tony Michaelides, had dropped in at Erasmus's flat to see the Factory team. It was lunch-time and Wilson was bunking off from Granada, and he and Alan were pleased to greet the professional side of the industry.

'Just wanted to know what this Joy Division thing is, a single or something?'

'Yes, we've got a new single out a week on Monday, "Love Will Tear Us Apart", it's called. It's fucking great. Wanna hit on this?'

'No thanks, Al. It's just that I've been doing the shops this week and every bloody shop I go into, the manager or the assistant has a go at me 'cause I'm from Manchester, and all they want to know about is this Joy Division single.'

'That's good,' said the boys.

'Good, it's amazing, every shop. I've not seen interest like this in a release for years. You've got a hit on your hands, guys.'

'Oh.'

And that's how it works.

When you think you've got a hit, you haven't. Wilson in particular was convinced that the previous JD single would do it. 'Dance dance dance to the radiooooooo'; oh my God, the DJs will love it – it's all about radio, it just has to go.

He had got so excited that he'd asked advice from a lady at Virgin, who had taken Orchestral Manoeuvres (and his partner and their designer Peter Saville) off his hands, for the name and number of the best plugger in town. The very best. He'd schlepped his way to London and an extremely nice apartment just off Portland Place, a brisk stroll from Radio One, and got the big man to agree to handle 'Transmission' for just two grand. He'd driven straight back up the motorway to a gathering of the partners at Martin Hannett's speakered-up flat to tell them the good news.

'Ummmmm,' said Rob.

'Ummmmm,' said Alan.

Peter was quiet; he was packing for his inevitable move to London.

If you look like Bryan Ferry and think like Yohji Yamamoto, you probably have to move to London.

'We don't treat music as a commodity; so we don't use pluggers,' said Martin.

'OK.'

Wilson didn't argue. The mood in the darkly lit room was clear. It was that easy. At least he didn't fight it. It was the way they made decisions.

He still insisted on pressing 10,000 of these fabulous little 7-inch singles with their exploding nebula, textured card sleeves. Great.

And that way, he got to see what 6,000 7-inch records look like in their wire mesh pallets at the pressing plant. Every month.

A fellow conspirator called Daniel had an equal number of a thing called 'Warm Leatherette' by his outfit, The Normal, in the next mesh pallet. Those went down significantly quicker than Wilson's.

Did he learn a lesson?

Did he fuck. A few years later, he found out what 100,000 embossed 12-inch sleeves looked like when he over-optimized on 'Thieves Like Us' by New Order. Those same sleeves went on to topple over in a Stockport storage shed and completely wipe out an old couple's caravan stored nearby, and ended up as an art object when sculptor David Mach used 80,000 of them to build Egyptian pillars on a Manchester dance floor.

So sometimes, great records don't sell. At first. But they infect. They seep into the water-table. They change the world. 'Transmission' and the *Unknown Pleasures* that preceded it were John-the-Baptisting for Joy Division for a good year before the releases of 1980; they were ploughing the ground and they were sowing the seed.

The news from Michaelides that Friday was news that the harvest would happen.

If anything, Ian's fucking-off detracted from sales patterns. With the interest in the music, imagine how the general public might have reacted to actually seeing the real thing.

If? Fuck 'if'. You can 'if' yourself up the arse in rock and roll till the lining of your anus bleeds. The TOP 'if' from this period was uttered by one of his fellow band members: 'If Ian had just got on that plane on Monday morning, he'd have fucked his way across America and never looked back.'

Now there's a deep and gloomy thought.

So the record releases, already paid for and in train, kept the momentum and, strange to say, none of them really thought about giving up. Maybe Ian had just upped the stakes.

If he could take it that seriously, so could they.

27
A NEW NAME FOR THE KHMER ROUGE

Rob summoned a meeting in a café in the middle of town. When Alan and Tony swung in, they noticed that as well as the drummer, guitarist, bass player and manager, there was this girl they vaguely recognized.

She was introduced. Gillian Gilbert. Steve's girlfriend. Of course. She'd got on stage and done a bit of guitar at a Joy Division gig at Eric's.

'We've decided to continue,' said Rob, a little portentously.

'We'll do the rearranged America trip as a three-piece but when we come back, Gillian will join and we'll be back to four.'

Wilson and Erasmus were surprised. Very.

Twenty-four hours later they were even more surprised. When they'd had time to think about it. 'Cause they'd both wondered about replacement lead singers. But. Fucking hell, Gretton's clever. Don't mess with the family. Don't answer a tragedy with the complication of an outsider. Probably Gretton's finest move. And Erasmus and Wilson admitted that they would never have thought of it.

'A girl singer, brilliant, it says new direction, couldn't be more different,' cooed Wilson.

'I'm not singing,' said Gillian.

'Well I'm not singing,' said Bernard. 'How can I sing and play guitar? I'm not fucking Roger Whittaker.'

'Well I'm not singing,' repeated Gillian.

'Well?' said Wilson.

'Keyboards; she plays keyboards,' said Rob, implacably.

'Well, I've got a keyboard; we just bought it. Seems quite easy. A lot of it's done for you, you know, you just press the buttons.'

'I don't mind singing,' said the keyboard player's boyfriend.

They all ignored him. He's a drummer and these people were far too worldly and hip to think that the lovely Phil Collins could ever be a valid role model.

The uneasy crown of the frontman was later to fall firmly on Barney's head but that was for later. For now, fucking get on with it.

'Great, you seem to have loads of ideas. It's going to be a very different Joy Division.'

'It's not going to be Joy Division. We all made an agreement when we started that if any member left the group we would have to change the name.'

'And I suppose Ian's left the group.'

'Looks like it.'

'So we're changing the name.'

'Well, that's something anyway,' said Alan, revealing for the first time perhaps his slight unease with all this post-modern cleverness and German shit.

'We're going to be called New Order.'

Great, great name, said Wilson. And the poor, sad fuck was sincere.

It wasn't until two months later that he found out 'New Order' was a common phrase, but one that had reared its head in *Mein Kampf*. He found this out on live TV, around 11.00pm on Channel 4's amateur half-hour–one-hour talk show, *Loose Talk*. He'd done his bit as revolutionary music entrepreneur and was relaxing into the studio sofa when suddenly this drunken, half-attractive woman, ex-editor of a national women's magazine, asked him pointedly how he liked making light shades out of babies' skin.

Wwwwhaat the fuck?

She called him a Nazi, explained the New Order connection and blathered on.

Wilson's position deteriorated shortly thereafter when in an effort to explain, he first put his hand on her knee and then began his justification with 'Listen, love.'

Northern familiarity can go down like a lead balloon south of the river in Deptford. He was fucked.

The next day he asked Rob, not angrily but forlornly, why this was happening to him again.

'I'm sorry, To, I got the name from a TV documentary I was watching. The Khmer Rouge had just changed their name to the "New Order of Kampuchean Liberation".'

Did he know that Wilson was a secret admirer of Pol Pot? Probably.

Wilson had liked Pol's Sorbonne background and the rational exactness of identifying that all revolutions are fought by the working class and won by the middle class. So taking out the middle class made sense. Liked the logic. Even if killing everyone who wore glasses was a bit black and white.

Did Gretton know this? Sure, the explanation appeased his mate. And his mate would get shit for it for the next several years. The irony: the situationist-anarchist media man with a Nazi tag. Maybe Rob loved irony; or just a wind-up.

And the Gillian thing wasn't the only heads-up brainfucker that Gretton came up with. He had another idea, which he broached that autumn at a general meeting to discuss the healthy sums of money that were about to flow from the 150,000 and counting copies of *Closer*, and the delicious way that the first album, *Unknown Pleasures*, was struggling merrily to keep up, playing catch-up with a dollar sign. And all this without advertising, or pluggers or marketing budgets. Fuck, it was funny. And funny was the right time for Rob to make his play:

'Let's open a club.'

'Wait on, Rob, me and Alan have been there, you don't want to do that.'

'Why not?'

'Cause when it's empty, *your* club, empty, it just really hurts. The Factory gave us more pain than joy, Rob.'

'He's right, Rob, it was very painful.'

'No, Alan, this won't be painful, it'll be full all the time, every night of the week. It's got to be open seven nights a week so no one has to go home. Did you know there's nowhere to dance in Manchester from Monday to Wednesday?'

They didn't know that, and Rob was hitting a nerve here. Of course, it was obvious, their wonderful city should have everything.

'And we'd be putting something back.'

Here it was, the final nail in all their coffins.

Putting something back.

Gretton's motives are lost in the mists of time. He, the most monogamous and faithful man in this group of dicks on wheels. (That epithet applies to about every other male in this story, though we need not go into detail. But apparently Factory folk had a bad rep. In LA, even). He, Rob, would often say he pushed for a club so he could ogle pretty girls. Other times, he would say he suggested the Factory/New Order business partnership knowing it was the only way he would get New Order's cash out of Wilson. But 'putting something back' – this was Wilson fodder. Getting it to happen.

Wilson's pet theory of that month, or was it week, was Keats's Aeolian harp theory. In one of his letters, Keats imagines the artist as the Aeolian harp, which is played by no musician, but rather the wind passing over the taut string. In some deformed piece of Marxist literary criticism, Wilson saw the power of punk and post-punk as being drawn out from the artist by the vibrant culture around him. The excitement and potential of the scene in Manchester since that Pistols gig had flowed around and over and through the members of Joy Division and had been part of the production of the music that had just made all this money, and hey, we're going to pay royalties to Manchester. Fantastic. Build our city a club.

And build the city a club like the ones they'd just seen in New York. This hit the mark too.

They had all just returned from their rearranged East Coast trip, the one Ian was meant to go on. Joy Division, A Certain Ratio, Gretton, Wilson and Hannett took up a three-week residency in Manhattan and East

Orange that autumn. Do gigs on the Eastern seaboard and record some tracks in a cheap studio in New Jersey.

For the trip, Wilson took a loft for his band A Certain Ratio on Hudson Street, above the Lo-Jan Cafeteria and next to the Citibank on Franklin, rented from a geezer called Chuck, which is another clue in the afore-mentioned pop quiz for Scorsese fans investigating the mystery at the heart of *The King of Comedy*.

Chuck?

Well, he was a loft landlord. And he was De Niro's loft landlord. Knew Robert well enough to explain how New York Italians hold their balls while they talk to you. Told Wilson Bobby had got him a part in his next movie. A Scorsese movie. He, Chuck, was going to play a rapist.

When Wilson called to pay him the rent, there he was, in makeup, and a Scorsese crew crawling all over his building.

Hey, Chuck's a star. My landlord's in the movies.

And guess what. The next Scorsese movie is *King of Comedy,* and there's no rape scene. Where's my fucking landlord? Oh, fuck, there he is in the back of shot. Answer to pop quiz. Chuck later plays the annoying barber who gets garrotted in *Goodfellas*.

That kind of finishes that excursion to Tribeca and takes us back up to Midtown. The three weeks saw the team spending a lot of time either playing or hanging out at Hurrah's at 62nd and Broadway, and Danceteria, then on 38th. Cool design. Clubs as venue and disco and style lounge all in one. The kind of clubs that David Byrne could go to the toilet in. Stylish. It was a couple of years before the heyday of the Garage and Fun Factory, which took New Order in other directions, but those first two were enough. They were cool clubs. And if New York had them, then why the fuck didn't Manchester?

The trip also featured the theft of New Order's gear van from outside their crap hotel on 44th Street.

Wilson had called, mid-morning, at the pit next to the Algonquin (ah, yes, the Iroquois), to get ACR's bongos back from New Order's van. Terry, chief roadie, was the only one awake.

'It was here last night,' said Terry, out on the street.

'What was here last night?' inquired Wilson.

'The van.'

'What do you mean, "It was here last night"?'

'It was here last night.'

'I'm sorry, Terry, are you saying that, here, where I can see a Cadillac parked by the kerb, that here, the last time you looked, which was at 3.00am, was our gear van?'

'That's exactly what I'm saying.'

'Fine.'

Fuck.

They didn't find the van in the towed-vehicle park down on the 40th Street Pier.

The Highway Patrol in Queen's found the van, empty and abandoned on the central reservation of the Long Island Expressway a couple of days later.

And the FBI found Steve Morris's drum kit, the one Hannett had made him reassemble on the opening day of the recordings for *Unknown Pleasures*, when they stormed a lock-up in Jamaica near JFK seven years later. It's just wonderful how things come round, isn't it?

So, van security had been questionable, but they'd loved the venues they played in. And Rob was now playing on that sense of 'I want, I want' common to all children, musicians and Mancunians. And his audience were all three.

It was probably less than ten minutes since he had first mentioned that word 'club', and already a great splish splosh of socio-cultural theory, distorted capitalism and unique Manc pride – New York's got one; well we better bloody have one – it's not that they thought 'fuck London', it's just that not even thinking about London SAYS fuck London… all this was making Fac 51 a real odds-on runner.

The only bet against was Martin. He'd come to this meeting to discuss a Fairlight. Or Farelite. Or something. To this day, his partners probably can't spell what it was Martin wanted to talk about. 'Cause the rush was all club club club.

Sorry, Martin.

What was it, a synthesizer? Oh. And a recording studio to put it into, uh-huh...

But a club! Paying Manchester the royalties it deserves... yaaayyyyyy.

Martin didn't sulk that morning. But he stared a little more intently than usual.

28
INDUSTRIAL FANTASY ON WHITWORTH STREET

The next few months were rather like preparing a dinner party. List the ingredients, if only mentally, source them and get them.

They would need a manager for this club.

Rob tried a local promoter out on a couple of New Order gigs when they got back from America. He did good. His name was Howard Jones, or Ginger. Wilson was unsure; mostly because Britain was covered with posters that autumn declaring 'HOWARD JONES?' To have a manager for their great venture who might be confused with some dodgy keyboard thing being promoted to fuck by some London record company was not the pure style that Wilson demanded. But Gretton liked him. And that was enough.

We must remember that at this point Wilson was a little in awe of Gretton. His decision not to take Joy Division to some Warner Brothers major label offshoot had created this little Starship Enterprise called Factory. Irrelevant that Rob's motives had been to 'do anything to avoid having to get on a train to London to go and talk to cunts'. Wilson saw Rob's decision as visionary and genius-proving. If he thought Ginger was the man, Ginger was the man.

And they would need a building for this club.

They looked at an old disused cinema on the north side of town in a place called Oldham Street. The dimensions were a little too defining. And then they looked on the south side of town and checked out the International Yacht and Marine Centre on Whitworth Street. A yacht show-room that was moving to new premises out in Salford Quays; more appropriate to be by the bloody water, obviously, and Salford Quays was the regenerated former Port of Manchester. Lots of docks and stuff like that.

The place on Whitworth Street was massive. The showroom space was a great rectangular box of a building. Two hundred feet long, 50 feet deep from the street façade and 60 feet high, with no floors. A toy box waiting to be filled.

At one end of the box was the Roundhouse, a semi-circular four-storey office building that wasn't for rent but had a basement that was empty and could fit a nice little cocktail bar. Just think, if they'd invented the phrase chill-out room ten years earlier we could have got really excited.

The big empty box was dominated by the very thing it was built for. Not yachts. Who intentionally builds a showroom for yachts in Manchester? No, this thing had been built in the 1920s by a steel stock-holding company. It was a warehouse for steel and it was held aloft by great H-shaped steel girders.

By the way, have we mentioned that warehousing was actually the big gig in our town? People tend to get misty-eyed about manufacturing and its decline. Were we the manufacturing centre of the British Empire? Were we fuck. We were the warehousing centre of the British Empire. We store it and we sell it; some other fucker has to make it. It's called added value.

And the boys decided to add value to this great echoing box of red brick with its steel-and-rivet theme.

And they would need an architect or something for this club.

Although Peter had gone off to London, he remained in charge of all matters aesthetic. He had reduced his partnership percentage from 20% to 5% in return for a pay-off of £15,000. This was to be provided in three tranches of £5,000 each, to be paid when he finished the next three jobs. Never mind what jobs. The idea was that since he would be stupidly late again, perhaps the dangling of a £5g carrot would speed the process and stop Rob arguing for a hit squad to be sent down the M1.

Did it work? You must be joking. Takes more than money to get Saville up to speed.

But he was up to speed on this club thing. Quite excited from his basement flat in Holland Park, and he told his mates that the club was to be designed by Ben. Ben Kelly from Appletreewick. How could one resist working with someone from Appletreewick?

No one questioned this decision. Peter said. So it happened.

We've discussed Gretton's role as a cross between Bradley Hardacre and Andy Warhol. Ben was simpler than that. He was Andy Warhol. At art college he had dressed and done his hair, even, in pure other-Factory style.

He and Peter had come together over a particular devotion to the art-maths conundrum of covering a space with the least possible material – that is, researching patterns of mesh or cut-out metal. The similarities between the steel cut-out front door that Ben had done for the new London offices of the Lynn Franks PR company and the blue-on-orange cut out sleeve for Orchestral Manoeuvres' first album on Dindisc Virgin (regular design classic that one, kids) were the start of a special friendship. And it was to take Ben of Appletreewick in the Yorkshire Dales back north to the great city of Manchester.

And they would need to decide what Ben was going to design.

Wandering round the shell of the building, the week that the last catamaran was decamped to the Quays, Wilson waved his arms in the direction of an underhang that ran along the long street side of the box.

'So we'll put the stage there and then this, the middle, will be the dance floor and we can put the main bar down the far end. Cool.'

And that was it.

It.

We need to explain here the political process that informed all decision-making in Factory Records and, as it happens, all decision-making in the Joy Division and New Order camps too. There was an absolute system of debate and negotiation. It doesn't have a name. Nor should it, 'cause it's completely bloody stupid. It's based around 'the majority of one'. If one person thinks or says something, then that's it. You don't debate it, you get on with it.

'Shall we put the single on the album?'

Desultory pause.

'Naw.'

'OK.'

And a decision that will cost 300,000 album sales is taken.

Just like that.

Let's call it the all-for-one-and-one-for-all system. Occasionally the idea itself was so strong that one lone dissenter did lose out; very rare, but this club thing had beaten Hannett's studio demands to pulp.

And the beauty of this system is that things happen without discussion and then for years to come, you can argue, debate and go nuts about the stupid fucking decision taken by this majority of one. You can have years and years of it. And they did.

Through the late eighties and early nineties, hardly a week or a Thursday management meeting would go by without a fifteen-minute harangue on the topic of...

'... and if we hadn't put the fucking stage under the beams on the side of the fucking building so that we could never re-book major bands because no fucking band can get its lighting rig on the bloody stage, we wouldn't be in the mess we're in now...'

'Yes, but if the stage had been at the far end it would have dominated the entire space and turned us into just a fucking venue and what...'

'Yeah, yeah, but what's the point of being anything if your fucking stupidity has bankrupted us and we can't bloody continue...'

Ah, Thursday afternoons.

Post-rationalization? Perhaps post-de-rationalization.

And they'd need to find the money.

Some of their own, some from a brewery, some from the banks. They put it together fairly quickly and then one day did the rounds of their backers, the breweries and the banks. Signing up.

At the second meeting, Wilson actually read to the second paragraph of the document he was signing. Must have been bored or something. He nudged Gretton. Whispered:

'Rob, this says I give a personal guarantee on the basis of my house.'

'Yeah, so what?'

'Well, I think I just signed a guarantee on the value of my house at that last place.'

'Exactly. Doesn't matter then, does it?'

'No, I suppose not.'

At the next three meetings to sign more papers, Wilson was now cool. When he saw the personal guarantee on his house, he just winked at Gretton. And signed.

Gretton smiled. He probably knew exactly what he was doing. Wilson probably didn't. But it was bloody exciting.

And this thing would need a name. Ah yes, a name.

It had a Fac number, that much was easy. They'd fallen into a peculiar, almost Babylonian obsession with numbering their stuff, these Manchester kids. That first release being Fac 2, not Fac 1 because Peter insisted his poster was number 1. OK, and hey, it's a double single so 2's good, isn't it, and then, the first album, well the gig at the Scala was 9 so it might as well be 10 and hey, 10's kind of an important number and albums are kinda important and then... then we're at 12 so this next Joy Division single, 'Transmission', is 13 and hey, it's time for a number for 'Love Will Tear Us Apart' and hey we're at 21, well since the last one was 13 we can make this one 23 and the album *Closer*, well, 25, a multiple of 5, hey that's cool and and and... Children at play. Having fun. Numbers ending in 1 had started being special projects; Fac 21 was the first Factory enamel badge. Cool. And this club project was 51. Fac 51. But it would need a name too.

It was everybody's task. But Rob did the business. He had gone home after an afternoon meeting where the absence of a name had been noted. And God knows why, but he'd picked up Wilson's little red book; actually, in this case, a big green book.

Part of the initiation process, the previous year, as this conspiracy got going, was to receive from Wilson a large green book, part funny, part fascinating, called *Leaving the 20th Century*. It was a collection of situationist works. Situationism's greatest hits. Yes, that Durutti Column thing again. As if anybody wanted to know about this obscure bunch of revolutionary French town planners from the fifties who had matured into the hard-but-hidden edge of student revolution in the late sixties.

Wilson, a situationist? Give me a break. He was just a fan. Been lucky enough to score acid at university from a couple of guys who were the main translators of Vaneigem and Debord. Connected with and fell for the sheer political fun of it. And of course bored all his mates rigid with the shit, including giving them all this book as a welcome-aboard present.

But that evening Gretton picked up the big green book.

And therein read...

Formulary for a New Urbanism

SIRE, I AM FROM THE OTHER COUNTRY

We are bored in the city, there is no longer any Temple of the Sun. Between the legs of the women walking by, the dadaists imagined a monkey wrench and the surrealists a crystal cup. That's lost. We know how to read every promise in faces – the latest stage of morphology. The poetry of the billboards lasted twenty years...

And you, forgotten, your memories ravaged by all the consternations of two hemispheres, stranded in the Red Cellars of Pali-Kao, without music and without geography, no longer setting out for the hacienda where the roots think of the child and where the wine is finished off with fables from an old almanac. That's all over. You'll never see the hacienda. It doesn't exist.

The hacienda must be built.

'We'll call the club the Haçienda.'
OK.
What a great fucking name.

29
YOU'RE ALL WANKERS

With around three weeks to go to opening night, the team went for a look around.

They walked through the building site of an entrance where the great wooden doors with their 5 and 1 cut-outs were leaning ready to be hinged up, over the shining, industrial steel flooring with its circular cut-in rush matting. And (and it's part of Ben's narrative-of-space genius), the whole place opened up for them in a flood of great pale blue walls – not any pale blue, but specific RAF and pigeon blue, on through the blue post-modernist arch, turning right into the great space, the great, enticing sprung maple dance floor ringed by black-and-white rubberized street bollards straight from Bologna. And the punctuation of the space was the great vertical steel girders, clothed in 45-degree stripes, some silver, some black, some yellow. The Haçienda had been built.

The guys are pleased, a little awed by their own shit. Except Martin. Very much the unimpressed onlooker.

'Buildings create synergy, see.' Wilson has his arms out. Those TV presenter gestures can be a bit much. He steps up onto the raised dance floor. 'They concentrate creativity. When the Victorians built railway stations, they didn't just put up platforms and a Portakabin. Buildings change the way people think. That's how it worked in Renaissance Florence.'

Martin had had enough. 'Yeah, but this isn't Renaissance Florence, this is dark ages Manchester.'

Wilson ignored him. 'It's beautiful, Ben. Thank you.'

'Hang on a minute,' said Martin. 'Is this real, are we really doing this? I thought it was some kind of trip. You've actually gone and built it. How much?'

'It was meant to be £500,000 but I think we've gone a bit over,' said Alan. 'It's all investment at the start but afterwards it's all profit. It was in the business plan.'

'£700,000,' muttered Rob, pulling on a joint.

'Well, now I know where my music budget's gone to. You realize we've got nothing in common. I'm a genius. You're all wankers. You'll never see me again. You don't deserve to see me again.'

Martin turned on his heels and out into the light of Whitworth Street.

The ones inside were still in the half-light. The Hac's vaulted glass roof sent in enough daylight to illumine the slightly dismayed faces.

Finally.

'Nice, though, isn't it,' said Wilson, getting back on track.

30
ANOTHER SETTING

And Martin wasn't the only one who jumped ship that spring.

Revenge fucking takes its toll. The only way to feel no pain is to feel nothing. Get cut off. Easy when Erasmus installs an old pinball machine in the back of the flat/office. You can stay all night just rolling joints and hitting those flippers with your second finger.

Wilson had even found (well, Erasmus had spotted it, of course) a great old three-storey Victorian house, untouched-up since the fifties, in a weird street that was part park, part cul-de-sac and part dual carriageway, in Didsbury, about a mile from the Palatine Road headquarters.

The cottage on the Moors had been sold.

She hadn't wanted the Victorian pile. Didn't even go and see it at first. She didn't want it.

She didn't want anything he wanted. Period.

And she didn't like the way it was all going.

'Fucking black. Fucking black fucking Factory, fucking death factory fucking black fucking death...'

He had brought back to the cottage a couple of rather obvious Conran hi-tech-manqué two-shelf video and TV racking systems. He'd just brought them in through the front door. They were indeed black. Which seemed to upset Lindsay. She explained why as she threw them both violently out into the street.

They weren't getting on.

Buildings are important, but not always in the way celebrated by Fac 51. How many dead relationships linger on? 'There's still this appeal that survives through the years' and all that bollocks.

And then, for all the depths of our great intangible emotions, a simple change of address, the simple act of moving your towels and toothbrush to a new bathroom and hey presto, the break is made. They say it's the same for heroin addicts. Which means it's probably true, because they are the two great addictions.

Moving means moving on.

She announced that she was going to London. Moving to London.

Some guy, probably her antique-dealer friend. But London? Just say no to London.

He hung on even as he drove her to the station.

'I'm asking you one last time, don't go.'

She smirked. Or maybe it was a smile.

She reached over with her hand to his face.

'Get your fucking hand off me. Get your fucking hand...'

She pulled her hand away.

'That's the last time you'll ever touch me.'

She reached over and touched his cheek again. Proving points.

'Now *that's* the last time you fucking touch me. Will you just fuck off.'

So she did, about three minutes later at the permanently cramped car-and-taxi rank that fronts Manchester Piccadilly station, the entrance to that long tunnel that takes you to London Euston and all those southern bastards.

She got straight out of the scrappy old Peugeot and walked erect, in and away.

Wilson sat in the car.

This, of course, is Manchester and no one mourns for long.

'Oi, move that fucking piece of shit.'

He was blocking a Cortina.

Wave of hand.

'Sorry, sorry... Fuck off.'

Wave becomes two fingers, the automatic gearbox engages, the wheel is turned and life goes on.

31
I'M SORRY, I'VE HAD A VERY LONG DAY

The band management stuff was going well.

That's called being facetious. Ironic.

It was shite.

Remember Simon from A Certain Ratio? He's giving up singing.

Vini, the greatest guitarist in the known world, is now out of his bedroom but he's taken up singing again.

Fucking hell.

Wilson, on a losing run admittedly, set about trying to get Simon singing again and get Vini not singing again. Let it be written, he failed miserably on both counts.

Bastard musicians.

But there's always the day job.

▶▶|

Sorry, did we mention that our hero had also lost his day job. Well, not the whole job. Just the new bit of the job that didn't involve interviewing farmers from North Wales who used geese responsive to their whistling to herd their sheep. Sheep-geese, not sheep-dogs. Those stories had become a piece of his past. He had been given a try-out as *World in Action*'s first designated on-screen presenter. Remember, that was where he was on the day of Ian's departure. Working for the daddy of all documentary programmes. And the mother as well.

He'd been doing OK. He'd had a spot of bother with the police over a 'cigarette' that they had retrieved after it had been ejected from a speeding maroon Peugeot on the Mancunian Way roundabout. Caused his bosses a bit of sweat, but he felt he was back in favour work-wise after Lord Denning, sitting in judgement on a controversial *World in Action* doco on the attempts by the government to wipe out the British Steel Industry, had described Wilson in the Court of Appeal as 'a dangerous human being who had set out from the very beginning of this programme to bring down not only Sir Derek Ezra, not only the British Steel Corporation, but Her Majesty's Government itself.' This for an interview that was hardly biting. Thanks, Lord Denning.

And then came a half-hour about two radical Cambridge economists. Wilson had actually seen the older one's dick.

The great thing about meeting Professor Wynn Godley wasn't just that he was as bright as the centre of the sun and then some. There was also the fact that Professor Godley was married to the daughter of the sculptor Epstein. As a lad, he had posed for his father-in-law. He had been the model for the great and naked bronze sculpture of the devil that hung above the side entrance to Basil Spence's Coventry Cathedral. You went there with your mum and dad. To a cathedral. And you saw this forty-foot Lucifer and his prick. The devil's prick. Good stuff, going out with your mum and dad.

And now Godley and his partner had run the new Tory prime minister's economic policies through their own model and were confidently predicting that if she went on as she intended there would be 5 million people registered unemployed by 1985. Five million unemployed. 'Impossible,' said the responsible press, 'these people are madmen.'

World in Action was investigating the madmen.

All the interviews and background shots were done. They were spending the weekend editing a twenty-minute film, and then they were holding a six-minute slot for an interview with Thatcher's chief minister (and Richelieu of the new right visionaries), Sir Keith Joseph.

That would be done on Monday lunchtime and slotted in.

Some time on the Saturday morning, Wilson lost it and turned on his producer in the cutting room:

'I'm sorry, David, I just don't agree with the way you're cutting this film. You're making a film about the long-term decline of the British economy, when we have in these out-cuts the real story that this bunch of mad fuckers are going to put millions of people on the dole. That's the film I thought we were making.'

David was a small geezer, clever, responsible, by appearances not given to the pursuit of pleasure. He was stoical.

'I understand you have a problem. I think you should go and talk to Ray and Alan.'

The two big bosses were in that morning. They were taking Monday night's show quite seriously.

Wilson knocked politely. These were big-time investigative journalists. Wilson couldn't investigate a bus stop. He just told stories to camera. He should have known his place.

But he didn't and blurted out his misgivings about the edit going on downstairs.

The odd couple were interested. Went downstairs and asked to watch the entire rough edit and then returned to their office. Ten minutes later David and our over-reacher were called in.

'We'd like Tony to be given till 4.00pm this afternoon to do his own edit. We'll watch that at 4.00pm, and then we'll know what we're talking about.'

Wow.

The rest went as if in a dream.

Wilson cut his twenty minutes. They watched. It screamed 'Five million unemployed in five years'. It had a headline. David was carefully but powerfully asked to stand back and let the lad finish the show. He was told he had no choice. Hurt, but he took it, praise him.

Late Sunday afternoon the finished piece was viewed, and Wilson was brought back up to the third floor and applauded.

'We're very impressed, very. We've been watching you for a while, we think you're perhaps more than just a reporter.'

Oh, God, thought Wilson, they're considering making me a producer, or at least making me something. *World in Action*. Oh God.

'And you'll get the train to London this evening and stay at the White House ready for the 10.00am prep for the Joseph interview?'

Drrrrrrrng drnnnnnnnng. Wake up. Dream over. Reality.

'Uuurgh, yes, well, no, Ray, it's fine. I'm going down tonight, but I'm not going by train, it's cool I'll be at Golden Square for 10.00am. We prep till 11.00am then it's straight to Whitehall. Easy.'

'But you should get the train, you must get the train.'

'No, no, listen it's fine. I'll be there. No problem. It'll be fine,' and he sidled out of the office.

Imagine the leather-topped dispatch box that runs down the central reservation of the House of Commons in the mighty Houses of Parliament. Imagine it cleared of all the books and boxes, empty, long and clear, except for a great triangular wall of white powder running like the great wall of China, only straighter, from one end of the table to the other under the Speaker's chair. Pacinoesque. The mother of all lines in the mother of all parliaments. This character in his baggy black Comme Des Garcons double-breasted is up on the table, crawling forward on all fours, alternately muttering to Sir Keith and then inhaling.

Imagine every few seconds, in a white fluorescent eye-spasm, the line of powder becomes a white line whizzing beneath your eyes as you're carried face forward down the M1.

Imagine it, because that's how some people imagine it. But it wasn't like that.

It was worse.

Wilson had not explained to his bosses why he couldn't get the train. There was no way he could carry five half-inch masters and a pair of big bloody multi-tracks. He was delivering the A Certain Ratio masters to Porky's cutting room in Portland Place, London, and the multi-tracks were needed by New Order in Trident round the corner. All booked in for 4.00pm on Monday afternoon.

And besides, the drive was so wonderful.

From Manchester to London by car is a brain fuck. First, you drive away from London, heading westerly, which is damn annoying. After twenty minutes of putting a few exhaust gases into Cheshire you hit the M6. And this starts the great black highway that is the M6-M5 travellator, which comes to a great grinding stop at the one place no one wants to stop. Birmingham. The irony in no way eases the hours sat in bloody queues.

But if you lived up in the hills, say, your point of departure was some little stone cottage up in the piece of Derbyshire that rises up to the Manchester horizon, then you could take off up and over the tops. In less than an hour you're hurtling down to a junction on the M1, and you just get on and motor. Great drive.

So it was easy. Set the alarm for 5.30am. Out of the door by 6.00am. Normal time for the journey? Three hours. Allow one more for problems. Granada, Golden Square, Soho, by 10.00am.

▶▶▶

He threw the tapes into the back, overnight bag in the front. Revved up and headed up Monk's Road, the steep and narrow lane that went over the tops and joined the road that would take him to the Chesterfield road.

6.05am. Excellent. It must have been about halfway up the hill that the long-wheelbase Peugeot's rear wheels started to spin. Fuck. They spun some more. Fuck.

Wilson looked out of the window. It was white. Outside the window was white. All of it.

Snow.

Snow? It was April. Bloody April. It doesn't snow in April. Please, Lord, it doesn't snow in April.

It doesn't except in a major freak storm every fifteen years, and the wait was up. It had happened. Correction, it was happening.

He made it over the top with a little slipping and a little sliding. It was slow going.

6.35am. He turned up onto the Baslow Road. Snow covered the road. He was about six miles into it when he came round a bend and there ahead of him a hill, drifts, jack-knifed lorries, stalled buses.

A three-point turn, and backtrack, gingerly, to Chapel-en-le-Frith and then through to Buxton a little further south. Not panicking yet. Take the lower road through to the north of Derby.

7.05am. Turn on to the A556. Cool.

7.16am. A hill; drifts, jack-knifed lorries, stalled buses. Jesus.

Retrace into Buxton. Panicking like hell now. Do joint. Wilson wasn't crazy about working stoned, just increasing the challenge and the adrenalin rush wasn't the point, but his nerves were going, he was now late. Definitely late. And the interview prep for a Cabinet Minister was serious stuff.

7.34am. Turn on to the A515. The Ashbourne Road, the lowest of the routes across and the most southerly. Hit the Derby Ring road from the South and whizz round to the M1.

7.42am. Another fucking hill, more drifts, more fucking jack-knifed lorries and stalled bloody buses. Oh my God. Accept that there is no route; this morning of all mornings there is no route over the Pennines that isn't bloody closed.

8.15am. Back in Buxton. Head west. Have we established that Wilson hated driving in the opposite direction? Well, now it really hurted.

'OK, OK, stay calm, have another joint, head over through Leek to Stoke-on-Trent.'

He was heading back to the bloody M6.

The radio was on, in case there were traffic warnings.

8.50am. Approaching the Stoke entrance for the M6. Traffic warning.

'The M1 is blocked from junction 15 to junction 14 outside Stoke.'

He stays on the side road. Does another joint.

9.20am. And still 160 miles from the capital, he eases round the roundabout and down the slip road to join the... stationary car park that is a gridlocked motorway. Fuck. He pulls over into the emergency lane and stamps on the brakes. Engages reverse and heads back up the slip-way. That's back up the slipway the wrong way. Neerrrr nerrr, nerrrr nerrr. Oh, it's a siren.

It took maybe ten minutes to calm the nice men in their dark blue outfits, acknowledge the crime, take delivery of some pieces of paper, and, being back on the roundabout, do a full circle and hit the A-road to Stafford.

It's 10.05am when our driver squeezes on at the next slip road. My God.

Isn't there a telephone or a clock or something in *Julius Caesar*, something that couldn't have existed in Roman times? We could have a mobile phone here and jazz it up a bit. But we're not going for that spot-the-archaism routine.

He hadn't rung in. Couldn't. Had to keep driving. Just keep driving. Just get there.

Over the next hour Wilson passes slowly through the Birmingham bottleneck.

He does a few joints to calm the jangled stuff.

His bosses do cartwheels.

At 10.30am, the team in Golden Square inform the bosses in Manchester that Wilson hasn't arrived.

At 11.00am the bosses in Manchester inform their bosses that Wilson has gone missing on the way to interview a cabinet minister.

At 11.30am the bosses' bosses inform their bosses that their *World in Action* reporter has gone missing en route to interviewing Sir Keith Joseph.

And has anyone heard from him?

Have they fuck.

11.45am. Corley Service Station just north of Coventry. Wilson parks up and runs to the phone. Dials Granada Manchester.

The other end: lots of noise and shouting.

His end: 'Don't worry, don't worry, just delay him, delay him, I'll get there, I'll get there.'

More noise and shouting.

No time for this, he's got to get there. Back in the car, back on the motorway. And back in a shitty fucking jam again. He gets off at the next junction. Calm now, just doing it. And pretty fucking stoned, it must be said, from the tranquillizing aids.

After a few detours in and out of Rugby town centre, we're on the M1 and rolling. Only two and a half hours late. Gonna make it.

12.55pm. Toddington Services, just thirty minutes from Hendon and the bottom of the motorway. Pull over. Hit the phone. Alan, his boss, in Soho Square.

Only a mite hysterical. Tells Wilson they're on the way over to the Ministry, have delayed the minister till 2.00pm. They'll set up and wait for him.

'And by the way, you're really fucking in trouble but get your arse here now and we'll worry about that later.'

Wilson ran back to the Peugeot, turned the key. Turned the key again. Turned the key again. It wouldn't fucking start. Annoying when your car coughs at you. In this case the moment was perhaps beyond bearing. Just too fucking much. Flooded. Immovable.

Think John Cleese. Think Austin Allegro. Think flailing that fucking inert piece of metal with a large branch.

Think quickly.

Wilson grabbed his raincoat. Did I tell you it was raining? It had stopped snowing. Hey! It was pissing down instead. Grab raincoat and briefcase of papers and run to the motorway entrance.

And stick out thumb.

Only forty-five miles to go.

1.05pm. The good news: barrister en route from Newport Pagnell to the capital in his Deux Cheveux stops, picks up Wilson and is so taken with his hard luck story he takes him all the way to Whitehall.

Bad news: this escargot-esque piece of French auto culture memorial-izes a time before Parc Asterix and Richard Rogers. It goes hand-in-hand with that other folded metal construction that allowed French males to piss in the street. That lunchtime the little Citroën might as well have gone hand-in-hand with a fucking pissoir, 'cause it could only do forty miles an hour. The primitive windscreen wiper had decided to go extinct and Wilson was forced to spend the next hour with his hand outside the car operating said wiper. Maybe that's why the guy stopped.

Arrival at the Ministry was greeted by panic and general hysteria from the *World in Action* crew. Calm down, calm down.

A less-than-pleased minister was wheeled in at approx 2.30pm, and after brief apologies the interview started.

Three good questions. Three good answers. Three minutes' screen time, two more to get.

But the fourth question involved the potential for Sir Keith and his dominatrix to wipe out British manufacturing and put millions on the dole.

Sir Keith, testily, gave a politician's non-answer.

That was it.

Wilson had had a hard day. A very fucking hard and a very fucking long day. And now this. He wasn't going to take it.

His supplementary was testier than the Minister. Just pissed off. And implying that, basically, like all politicians, he was a bleeding liar and could he please get on with it.

The minister exploded.

Wilson exploded.

Three minutes of poisonous argy-bargy ensued.

Wilson may even have mentioned that this is why Sir Keith had acquired the nickname 'Mad Monk'. Whatever it was, you might say it was unpleasant.

Behind the cameras, shock, bewilderment, dismay.

Finally, it all calmed down. Composure was regained. Two more good questions; two more reasonable answers. They had their five minutes down. Cursory goodbyes and insincere thank-you's were swapped.

The Minister left, Wilson's producer raged, and the film left for the labs at the same speed Wilson ran out the door to find some way back north to the Peugeot stranded at Toddington Services and the master tapes therein.

Jeeesus. Close call.

But the show was in the bag and no one would know any different.

Except.

Except that the occupants of the sixth floor back at Granada TV had been so consumed by the panic of the morning, that come 5.30pm when the processed film interview was sent up the line to be included in the finished piece, every one of Wilson's bosses watched the material. The uncut material. The whole damn thing. Wilson's exasperated chiefs watched in horror as their reporter got into a 'fuck you' slanging match with the most powerful man in Thatcher's cabinet. Oh, dear.

'We don't think you're really cut out for this,' said Mr *WiA* a week later, and that was it. Back to local loonies, mate, and those interminable debates in the corridors of Granada.

'That's it, Charles, no more, no fucking more. I have just spent this morning interviewing a dwarf who washes down the elephants at Chester Zoo.'

'He's a midget,' said Charles, trying to be helpful.

'That doesn't matter.'

'It does to him,' said Charles, a little hurt by this.

'I'm a serious fucking journalist, Charles, this is it...'

The long moan was interrupted by a three-month contract *Coronation Street* shooting star who, seeing Wilson in the corridor, began grinding and cooing her next single.

'What do you think, Tony?'

'Great, great, we'll sign you up tomorrow.'

With as much enthusiasm as a cat for a dog.

Oh, the irony of it all.

By the way, pop quiz: how many people unemployed by 1985? You've guessed it. A fuck more than were at the Last Supper.

32
SOUS LES PAVES
LA PLAGE

Oh what a fucking mess.

Career prospects in the toilet. Wife gone. Hannett gone. Ian gone. Absence was everywhere. And there was worse to come.

One week after his ejection from *World in Action* there was a band meeting round at Wilson's Old Broadway rooming house. Are there any words more dreaded in the world of rock and roll? 'Let's have a band meeting.' There are no more dreaded words in the world of rock and roll.

And the band in question were Section 25, Factory's Blackpool outfit. Sort of Post Joy Division intensity stuff. I think we've mentioned melancholia. And they were intense. And really fucking arrogant. And they managed themselves. Arrrgggggggghhh. Garlic and crosses are not enough when faced with bands who manage themselves. Carry a gnarled wooden stake and hammer it up their arseholes and into their spines. And don't work with them.

That night they sat in Wilson's front room and moaned. And moaned. Several hours. Gretton stayed comatose, Erasmus went with the flow, but Wilson listened and tried to talk to them. And they moaned some more. Loss of wife and partner, death of genius and career; the fragile spirit had survived all but not this, a long night's whinging by a band who manage themselves. As Blake put it, 17 April, 1982, between 9 and 11 in the evening. Despair.

Wilson's hopes and dreams went into hibernation for a while. A dark summer he had of it. He still walked upright, but there was maybe a 2-degree forward tilt now. The pressure, the pressure.

He was walking with this 2-degree tilt across Manchester's Albert Square, the big public jobby outside the Town Hall. OK, so it wasn't Tianenmen, but they'd done a fair job of pedestrianising. The sets were actually quite European. Wilson's favourite corporate claim of the entire situationist student event was 'sous les paves la plage'. Pick up the paving stones from Haussman's great imperial avenues and beneath you'll find sand. Throw the paves at the French riot police, and you'll find the beach.

No beach under these bastards, he thought. Yes, he was very, very, down. His thoughts were suddenly interrupted.

'You'll be back, To.' A voice, a shout.

Wilson stopped and turned round. A young-old tramp, sitting on one of the benches right in front of the town hall was smiling directly at him.

'You'll get back on top, T, mark my words. It's who you are. You WILL be back.'

Wilson walked towards him. Dressed in a tattered heavy overcoat, he looked ill. And lost, of course. But he was smiling.

They had a conversation about fate and life and about how things do turn round. His name was David. Over the years to come, up until maybe 2000, Wilson would see Dave on the streets of Manchester, give him his spare change and they'd smile and talk. David's smile was immense, coming from deep inside but then screened on a face that would some-times look healthy and sometimes look close to death or withering.

Twenty minutes of this first meeting and Wilson headed back off across the square leaving a smile that did not fade. Dave did not come from Cheshire. And Wilson realized he had just met his Boethius.

It doesn't matter if you don't know what *The Consolation of Philosophy* is, but as we never tire of saying, and you must certainly by now be weary of hearing, you should probably read more.

Because I don't trust you to read more, I'll explain that this great book was written in Quattrocento Florence by a great man fallen on hard times, with wife and children killed, fortune sequestered, and arms and legs in great heavy chains.

'It is my view that History is a wheel. Inconstancy is my very essence says the wheel. Rise up on my spokes if you like but don't complain when you are plunged back down into the depths. The good times pass away but then so do the bad. Mutability is our tragedy but it's also our hope. The worst of times, like the best, is always passing away.'

Was that Boethius, or was it David? It kept our hero going. The Consolation of Philosophy. Or the idea that there'll be another bus along in a minute.

PART TWO

33
OPENING NIGHT

piecetocam

F. Scott Fitzgerald has this thing about how American lives only have a first act. No comeback stuff. But this is Manchester. We do things differently here. We have second acts. This is the second act.

Some people say the opening night of the Haçienda was empty. That's crap. The opening night was packed; it was the next five years that were empty. Sometimes it was better that way. Better empty for the art when the only art was the look and the sound was well down the list.

It's fair to say that the opening night crew – Manchester's finest, half a hundred Londoners who knew what was going on plus a scattering of celebs from Leeds, Liverpool and Leith – got in the way of the décor. Too many people to get a full-on view of those wonderful pale blue walls, of the serried banks of gelled fluorescents on carefully chosen surfaces. Couldn't see the concreted-in cat's eyes, the forty-seven of them that lined the dance floor, for all them fuckers dancing. Good night, though. Alan took a back seat. Being anywhere, stationary, for more than ninety seconds had become a problem for Alan. St Vitus' dance, Wilson's mother might have called it. He was here, he was there and he was sort of never really anywhere, driven to the next thing which then became the past thing. Doing normal stuff was becoming a rarity. So Gretton and Wilson weren't too worried when he rang to put his forty-three friends on the door and was inconclusive about when he himself would put in an appearance.

Saville arrived at 4.30pm from London. Still Bryan Ferry. Does nothing change?

'Sorry I'm a bit late, guys, here's the tickets for tonight.'

'For tonight – tickets. This is tonight.'

'Yes, but I had a bit of trouble; do you like the one as an H steel girder?'

'Yes, it's fantastic but we open tonight and they're too late.'

'Maybe you could use them as souvenirs...'

This exchange sounds like fiction – natural in what many may assume to be a work of fiction. I mean, it's the same stupid conversation that Wilson and Saville had four years earlier in the Russel Club. And the same solution; yes, it can be a souvenir and Gretton mellows and Wilson beams, as if it was his idea, and revels in the sheer visual dynamics of his mate's vision. In this case it was the creamy but deep blue, a shade he had never seen or imagined, which took his breath away and then returned it in a purr.

'Great, we'll give them out as souvenirs of an historic night.'

Yes, it happened. Again. And on and on in time. Like we said earlier, if Peter had done the cover of this book, you'd have been given it as a souvenir on the night the book tour rolled into your town. The wheel is not to be escaped. Change is illusory.

Mostly.

Naw, fuck, entirely.

Opening night was crazy. This piece of industrial fantasy street was perfect for parties. Nooks and crannies, a narrative of space, taking you to the balcony via Ben's joke post-modernist arch, up and down the corridor that took you behind the games room to the basement cocktail bar. There, that dates you. Cocktail bars. Early eighties, mate. Shame they had a comeback in the late nineties.

And that wasn't a games room you shuffled past. Sorry about that. Pong had mutated into large stand-up Sega consoles by '82 and here was some extra revenue the guys were well up for. So the space on the left of the entrance was to be the games room. Until two weeks to opening.

'Where's the cloakroom?'

'The what?'

'The cloakroom, the fucking cloakroom.'

'What's your problem?'

'We don't have a cloakroom. We have special polished South African granite bar-tops that we haven't told Erasmus about 'cause he has a thing about apartheid, we have a balcony balustrade made of shaped QE-fuck-ing-2 mahogany, but we seem to have built an entire club without a cloakroom.'

'Fuck.'

Hence you did not pass the games room but the cloakroom, the only cloakroom in Manchester with forty-two power points. If you ever wanted to do a bit of ironing, these people were there for you.

And if you ever wanted to do a bit of irony? Ryan, the writer of bad prose about rock groups, turned up. He'd got his invite from his news desk.

It was early, the first crowds just filtering in.

Nice, you could see the walls.

'Mr Wilson, could I ask you a quick question?'

'Yes, Ryan.' It was opening night. Bon homie, even to this cunt.

'Who exactly have you built this place for?'

Sudden sharp shot of mental pain. Recognition of good question. Particularly good question, as it was a new question. Never asked themselves that question, had they?

Bluff it out. Stock answer.

'For the kids.'

And Wilson meant it. If they had ever asked themselves who they were building it for, they would have said the kids, surely.

'Have you seen the kids recently, To'? Have you? They're still going to dirty basements like Rafters and wearing grey raincoats. You've built a glossy New York nightclub.'

For all our ranting about the low esteem in which the world should hold people of the journalistic bent, this was interesting. Mostly 'cause it was true. Wilson was ready. He had the mouth and the brain. He replied.

'Oh.'

'Cause that was pretty much how he felt at that moment. Maybe when Eve gave Adam the look and then the apple and he sank his teeth in, maybe God said, 'Oh.' It would be a bit bloody boring if we had it all planned. God too. Let's hear it for free will and a glamorous New York nightclub in a grotty city in northern England.

It would have been nice if the invited guests had said 'Oh' when the very special guest came out on to the stage to declare the club officially open. The special guest was Bernard Manning – a large, obscene, allegedly racist comedian who had a national reputation for being the most obnoxious and politically incorrect laffmeister on the planet.

He had been chosen 'cause this was the Haçienda and the guys had decided to wake a few buggers up. Manning was a semi-national institution. Would take the piss out of anything and had developed a reputation with the liberal middle classes as a racist. For the uninitiated, he made Archie Bunker look like Ghandi.

The emergence of Bernard into this swirling arena of hip had the desired effect. One second's shocked silence. Thirty seconds' high-pitched booing, yelling, profanity and abuse. The attendees were shocked and angry. They screamed at the big man on the little stage.

After an eternity...

'Why don't you shut the fuck up?' said Manning.

That trebled the abuse volume levels.

'Fuck you,' said Bernard, entering into the spirit of it all.

'Fuuuuuuuckkkkkk youuu,' they screamed back.

'Bloody shit PA,' said the man from the Embassy Club.

Sidestage, Hooky put his head in his hands. 'Bernard Manning is taking the piss out of our sound system. This can't be happening.'

Mr Manning took another ten seconds on the chin. He used to give it, so he took it. If you ever went to his club in north Manchester, there was one rule: never get up to go to the toilet. The man will kill you. Kill you.

So he took it and then, with an imperial 'Fuck you all', wandered off stage.

Gretton and Wilson were pleased. An event. This was Manchester.

Afterwards, in the basement party, Wilson offered Manning a white envelope.

'What the fuck's that?'

'Three hundred pounds, Mr Manning. Your fee.'

'Fuck the fee, I didn't do anything. Keep it.'

This was Manchester.

34
A BOWL OF FLOWERS BY FANTIN-LATOUR

Late afternoon in Prestwich, north Manchester, round the back of a small Woolworth's, a few dozen yards off the main street. A large, low-ceilinged room, the low light levels mirroring the coming dusk that came in through no windows. New Order's rehearsal room.

It was a gathering. To discuss the next New Order album, the artwork, the campaign, the whole damn thing.

'Jesus, look at those stools, those are Alvar Aalto stools,' said Wilson, a little annoyed, a little amused.

Wilson had coined a line for the press who were now having a go to the Haçienda's low attendance levels. He would say, 'We give Alvar Aalto stool to kids in the street.'

They did. Honouring the youth of their town they provided décor that a £20-a-martini fleecing parlour could not have amortized. They had bought eighty low Alvar Aalto stools for the alcove and cocktail bar seating. Also, twenty tall numbers in the same bent bleach wood classic style. Extremely expensive and brought in from Finland at equally great expense.

And in the first twelve months, ninety per cent had disappeared. Compared to the catastrophic damage done every other week to one of the toilets just off the main dance floor – the level of masonry demolition going deep into the floor implied the use of a full-size pneumatic drill – the loss of a bunch of stools was incidental.

The fact that thirty-two then turned up in New Order's rehearsal room was therefore coincidental. If you couldn't join the public in stealing from your own club, what was the point of opening it?

Saville was holding forth. For *Unknown Pleasures*, Joy Division had brought *him* their ideas: a maths book with a diagram of the radar signals from a dying pulsar. Peter had taken their chosen image and placed it. Placed it in the centre of a black square. Placed it with utter perfection. But that was the last time they ever had the time or inclination to give Peter the visual push. From then on they were too busy gigging, recording or dying and Peter himself would come up with the visual ID and, as on this greying late afternoon, he would present it to the group.

'This is a painting of a bunch of flowers in a vase by Fantin-Latour from the National Gallery.'

Actually, it was a postcard of the Fantin-Latour painting from the National Gallery. Small and passed around the assembled crowd, seated on their low ex-Haçienda stools.

'Very nice,' said everyone, without caring much. Peter did the art. 'Get on with it' was the order of the day.

'Very nice.'

'Oh and there's one other thing,' said the image guru. 'I have been asking myself a question and I want the sleeve to answer the question.'

'What's the question, Peter?' asked Hooky, always willing to move the conversation along and show a little more interest.

'How many colours does it take to replace language, to replace the alphabet?'

People were beginning to doze off at this point, but Wilson had an edgy feeling. Colours. Special colours. Pantone fucking colours. Most people print colours by the four-colour printing process – that cyan, magenta crap. And Factory did that. But every so often Peter or one of his acolytes – for Peter had been followed by a trail of other 'great graphic designers on the way up' – asked for a special colour. Which meant the printers did the four-colour run and then added one, two or more runs for these 'special colours'. 'Cause Factory's designers did not trust the cyans and magentas to get together specifically enough to give them the exact bloody shade that their vision demanded. And since the music was great, then the packaging in which the customer received said art would have to have the same attention to perfection.

It cost more, to cut it short.

And Peter's intriguing question was bound to cost more. The explanation was almost mundane compared to the preceding analysis of cost, process and attitude. With ten colours representing digits zero to nine, you could make numbers one to twenty-six and reflect a Western European alphabet.

So that was that, they'd have this bloody picture of a bunch of flowers and some colour coding instead of lettering. Sounded good. No one complained. No one ever did. Peter was good. That was enough.

Conversation became desultory. Peter got up and began to wander. Wilson watched him walk, watched him walk towards the back left of the room, a jumble of desks, tables, and wires and wires and wires. Wilson had a stilled shudder of expectation. He knew something was going to happen, something was going to detonate, as Peter walked towards Steve and Gillian's corner.

The wires that hung all over Steve and Gillian's corner like some overgrown liana in a Tarzan movie, were not just wires. They were, like Steve and Gillian, connected. They were connected to a couple of primitive computers – early Apples – and also a pile of keyboards and synthesizers salvaged from the seventies. Wired up in pure Heath Robinson fashion, which is an old English phrase that I think means higgledy-piggledy (which is an even older English phrase). Soldered in, wired up, plugged through, stuck in; connected.

Today you can buy a silver box from Yamaha for £300, where all this stuff is done on one slim motherboard. Yesterday, someone had to find their way to the new instruments, the new way of making music sounds. It was probably going on in bedrooms across the developed world. But here we watch it in the little open-plan workshop that belonged to New Order's drummer and his girlfriend. Did they know the possibilities buried in these first-generation PCs? Or was it exploration for its own sake? Like the MGM lion was always saying.

There was a clue in pre-history, around four miles away. Take a line south-south-west across the city centre from New Order's Cheetham Hill base, take it for about four miles and you come to the campus of Manchester's grand red-brick Victorian university. Focus in on the physics department, pull back thirty-three years, and we're in at 1950. The guys here have just beaten the wankers in Philadelphia and Cambridge to inventing the computer. Easy peasy. 'We kept entering the numbers and they started a mad dance... nothing was ever the same again.'

Nothing was ever the same for poor Alan Turing, the gay genius mathematician who invented the idea of the computer. In his thesis of 1936 entitled 'Can all problems be solved in the end?' Turing proposed a machine, a universal machine, an imaginary typewriter-esque machine, that would process commands in a step-program mode. The world woke up. Fuck Babbage and his mechanical calculator. This would change the world. If only. If only there was such a thing as a synthetic memory. For Turing's machine required memory and in 1936 that was something that was locked in the homo sapiens' cortex.

We're not forgetting Steven and Gillian here, just getting their predecessors sorted and placing them in context. Basically, our boy Alan Turing went to Bletchley Park, solved the Enigma code with his mates, fucked Hitler and the U-boats and when the war ended embarked on the search for the memory that would unlock his universal machine. As did the other hustlers in Philadelphia, Manchester and Cambridge.

As you know, 'cause you've been reading this book very carefully, the Manc boys, Williams and Kilburn, won the race; they backed the cathode ray tube – a memory that sported 2,048 little bloody dots – and they got it right. Alan Turing's mob in Teddington, somewhere in the south of England, who cares where, got closed down, having taken the failed mercury-delay line route. Alan was moved to Manchester by the government. This was forty years before Flesh night at the Haçienda and a gay genius was hardly the hot item in Manchester at that point. Alan was an outsider in the world of Manchester's successful computer department. But at least he was able to play with the machine that only he had had the vision to imagine.

He sent out detailed workings to all his friends about the 'Baby' – for so, delightfully, was it named – and the baby's babies, the follow-up machines. He suggested to his chums that anyone caring to write a 'program' for the Manchester machine should do so and come up and try it out. One friend, the head of maths at Harrow, a big-time public school famous for being near where Elton John was born, wrote back and said he had a program.

'Come on up.'

Mr Strachey arrived on the train from Euston, as do most things that come to Manchester.

He spent the morning typing his program into a punch-card, for this indeed was the input method of 1950. All bloody morning.

And then the engineers, scientists, mathematicians and hangers-on stood back, and waited. Mr Strachey let his friend Alan insert the card.

'Deeeerrrrrr, deeerrrrr, der der derrr derrrrrrrrrrrr,' sang the computer.

God Save the bloody Queen. More shocking than the Pistols' jubilee work-out. 'Cause this was thirty cubic feet of valves and tubes and metal. And it was playing music. Kraftwerk, in what room or womb were you that lunchtime? The dawn of electronica was that moment.

Later that day, the machine gave a startling rendition of Glen Miller's 'In the Mood', for it was that stage in the evolution of the popular song. And thirty odd years later, New Order were trying to make what had been dubbed in 1950 'the electronic brain' do even more with music. Hannett had introduced them to the digital world with his AMS machine. Steven had added an early model of digital drums, a couple of round grey things, perched above the high-hat. Listen to Joy Division's 'She's Lost Control': tschh-tschhhh, tschh-tschhhh. The sound of twin synapses snapping.

And the experiments continued through the death of band one and the birth of band two. Sorry to make you play the records again, although if this book has any other point it eludes me, but go to 'Isolation' on the second and final Joy Division album, *Closer*. The journey that ends in DJ heaven has already begun.

And it is the junction of two roads that is destination. Rock and roll has always been 'Africa saying hello to Europe'. It has always been the sacramental sparking of rhythm and melody. Separate functions of the sounds that delight us, coming tightly together. Some guy said of ragtime that the left hand is in Africa and the right hand is in Europe. Couldn't have put it better.

And until the early 1980s these two functions had come together but not merged. A finger plucked and a string vibrated at a certain melodic pitch, while a stick hit a skin and a sound was made that formed a beat. But what the computer was to bring was the moment when a single piece of notation, a single clicked computer moment, would contain both rhythm and melody. That was the possibility, that was the new. That's what was being sought in the far back-left corner of New Order's rehearsal room.

Check out 'Everything's Gone Green', the New Order song that was the last they did with Hannett before the Haçienda 'You're all wankers' break-up. Tell me you can't hear it. Tell me you can't hear the world changing and the world arriving.

It was just five months before this darkening afternoon with Saville preparing the artwork for *Power, Corruption and Lies*, the new album, and walking, inexorably, towards the final packaging moment.

The group had used their primitive computers to get over a major problem. They didn't do encores. Sometimes. Well, sometimes they did and sometimes they didn't. But they didn't want to have to and they were tired of the fucking audience screaming and applauding as the last chord was hit and they ran off stage. So predictable. So mundane.

So now this computer stuff. Surely we can make something with the computer that we can leave switched on and it can just go on and on and on until they're all bored to death and fuck off? So they made it. Barney wrote some lyrics about a ship in a harbour and treating me like you do and they had two tracks: 'The Beach' and 'Blue Monday'. The single for this particular release. 12-inch only, 'cause as I said, it was fucking long.

And Saville stared down at the work bench, and stared down at wires and the confusion and the strange black square.

Wilson knew Saville had never seen a 'floppy disk' before. And this, remember, in a world where floppy meant floppy and hadn't been viagra'd up in to some sort of cool black cartridge. No, these ones were real floppy. Five-inch square, thin black cardboard containing something you never looked for inside but visible through those three crazy cut-outs. The cut-outs.

Peter picked up his first floppy and fell in love. Of course. Wilson knew he had his single sleeve now as well as his album sleeve. And he fell in love with Peter all over again, 'cause this record company stuff was just so much fun.

35
THE PROFIT AND LOSS

The men were bringing up the big cardboard boxes, up the flight of stairs into Alan's flat, the Factory offices. Lots of cardboard boxes with the stamp Fac 73 on the side. 'Blue Monday'.

Alan was tapping away on a calculator. The old flat was one place he could relax. And use the Olivetti calculator with the heat printing.

'Tony, have you done the maths on this release? Did you stop for one minute to work it out? I reckon that with the three special cut-outs, the four special colours and the silver inner sleeve on top plus the pressing costs, every copy we produce will cost us 79p. I've checked with Rough Trade and Pinnacle, our average return will be 81p per copy.'

'Yeah.'

'Which leaves us with 2p profit.'

'Yeah.'

'Which we split fifty-fifty with the group.'

'Yeah.'

'Which leaves us with 1p profit.'

'Yeah.'

'Out of which, according to the deal you did with Rob, we pay the publishing.'

'Yeah.'

'Which is 4½p.'

'Yeah.'

'So we lose 3½p for every copy we sell.'

'Exactly, exactly, but, first, it's a thing of beauty and second, Alan, we're not going to sell any, so don't worry. New Order are still underground and this is a 12-inch, for fuck's sake, not a pop single. It's like a dub-reggae-remix format, rare stuff. How many are we going to sell? Fuck all. And what's 3½ times fuck all? It's a small price to pay, Al. And I was thinking of you as well. Since they're going to be crowding up your flat for the next six months, they had to look beautiful, didn't they? And they do. Ahhhhh, just look at that,' he said, opening one of the boxes and turning the piece over and over in his hand.

The arrogance of it.

The music industry may be a crawling hive of hucksters, hypsters and whores. But it has one central glory. One crowning fact. The song. It is about the song and in the end only the song. And great songs cannot be stopped. Cannot be denied. 'Blue Monday' was not to be denied. Bam bam bam bam. How does it feel? How does it feel to be the biggest selling 12-inch in the history of the UK record industry?

Which it inexorably became, and we hope you saw that coming.

How does it feel? It feels great. And how does it feel to lose 3½p a copy? It feels great.

You can't put a price on irony.

36
HALLOWEEN

Of course, it would have helped if the club was making money. But it wasn't. It most certainly wasn't. Howard Jones, the manager, kept assuring the boys from Factory and New Order that everything was alright and the reason that they had to keep sticking their hands in their pockets was just temporary cash flow crossovers. That it had nothing to do with the fact that we were opening six nights a week, of which five were quieter than the City Art Gallery after closing, and were doing things like giving all staff taxis home at the end of each night. After twelve months, the Factory accountant explained that they'd been running an all-night limo service to every bloody party and shibeen in the north-west of England. And at last, fourteen months in, and about half a million pounds too late, belts were tightened. Opening was restricted to four nights a week. But Ginger was still the boss. Wilson was uptight, but Gretton held firm. And Wilson was confused. It was Gretton's genius in not going to London and signing to a major that had created this wonderful rollercoaster, so how could this genius be wrong about his chosen Hac manager?

When the axe fell, it was Gretton who wielded it. Who else? And it is an illustrative tale, so here shall we illustrate it.

'Twas Halloween. Wilson had had the staff collect dead leaves from the city parks and cover the inside of the club with them. And on that day, as we prepared for the dead to rise, Ginger went on the offensive against Wilson's removal campaign. Called a crisis meeting. Only the fifteenth that autumn, which was cool. The central thrust was that Ginger blamed the black hole, down which New Order's and Factory's cash were flowing, on the absence of a marketing and promotions manager.

'We have to have a promotions manager. We have to bring someone in,' said Howard, with absolute, unsmiling commitment.

'Howard, we have no money, we have less than no money 'cause we have no money and we're losing money on top of that, and you want us to add another cost to the payroll. You must be joking.' Wilson was semi-fierce. At least pissed off and hard-line.

'If we don't employ a marketing man now this club will never be a success.'

'We are not going to add any more costs and that's that. I'm sorry.'

Short meeting. Rob, silent. Alan, pensive.

That night, the board made up perhaps sixty per cent of the attendees for the Hac Halloween night.

They sat around in the upstairs salon of the Gay Traitor cocktail bar.

And Rob started.

'Howard, you know that when we started this thing a couple of years ago, you said that if you ever lost faith in the club working you'd resign.'

'Yes, Rob.'

'And this afternoon, you said that if you didn't get a promotions manager, the club would never be a success.'

'Yes, Rob.'

'And Tony told you there was no money and there would be no promotions manager.'

'Yes, Rob.'

'And therefore the club will never be a success and so you'll have to resign.'

'... yes, Rob.'

For the first time in this automated conversation, Ginger, on a roll and happy having exerted his ego at the afternoon meeting, gave a slight pause to consider the way the conversation was going. This was like taking a slight pause when your rowing boat gets to about three feet from the top of Niagara Falls. Good to take stock, but probably too late.

Gretton got up immediately and, with a smile, said to the assembly: 'Well, Ginger's resigned and I suppose we'd better tell the staff.' And Rob stalked off from bar to bar to reception to dressing rooms and proceeded to tell all the staff. No way back. No way at all. Not sure if Ginger's mouth hung open. Probably. Shellshock. Over. Done with.

Ginger was a nice guy. Wilson long regretted the way he had treated him, but in all the chaos and humour of their story, the one truly bad thing this little bunch had a habit of doing was empowering people beyond their natural level and then leaving them to live in a foreshortened universe. Not nice. Not intentional, but not nice.

For the record, Ginger was replaced by a committee of really good people. And as we all know, a committee of really good people is always a fucking disaster too. Just for the record. But one member of that committee was to bring on a major sea change in our story and we should here bring the boy in properly by taking us all to the match...

37
THE BEAUTIFUL GAME

Manchester is a tale of two cities – at least, of one City and one United, the two football teams who alternately grace and disgrace this city on the western foothills of the spine of England.

In the end, all sports are no more than a collection of numbers and words. The rules, the dimensions. All can be written down. All are written down. It's all there is. And within those precise specifications, human beings get on with it and there, in the gym, in the stadium, in the pool or field, a dramatic narrative is worked out with attendant visuals and emotional identification.

For better or worse. And for the very best, the numbers and words written down in the dark satanic mills of Oxford and Cambridge in the mid-nineteenth century provide the world with its favourite physical drama.

I know that our anti-hero has a habit of mentioning the fact that he went to one of these great knowledge pots, but this reference is merely pointing to a truth, and one that many may find shocking. All those bleeding-heart lefty liberal idiots who thought the working classes invented football, when of course in the days organized sport was invented the working classes weren't allowed to play sport of any kind 'cause they worked (that's where the bloody name comes from) six days a week; and on the Sabbath, well, sport was simply not allowed.

Shrove Tuesday, they ran around with a bladder and that was it. Compared to those incredibly leggy ladies who adorn Mardi Gras in Rio on the same day, it may not seem much. But from running and kicking and punching with a bladder grew something that is, at least until Ronaldo and the Stade de France, even more important to Brazil than their great women. And let's give Oxford and Cambridge their due, 'cause Wilson went to Cambridge after all and that is the standing joke in this dutiful novelization.

Pissed off with some public school git who picked up the ball with his hands and ran with it – typical cheating arrogant fucking public school bastard thing to do, isn't it – the football folks at our ancient universities codified their sport. The goal will be eight yards wide and eight feet high, etc. etc. Bleeding, right-on genius. A bunch of words and numbers, numbers like eleven, forty-five, two, ten; words like goalkeeper, penalty, free-kick; all the stuff that goes to create 'the beautiful game'.

And one of the beauties of the beautiful game is the ability of this special recreation to filter into man's great requirement for family. The great need to be part. To be part of your family, your village, your tribe, your country, your race, your world. Connect, we all want to connect. And the shared emotion of watching these numbers and words being acted out is quite simply beyond compare.

To really be a Catholic you have to be an Italian, and you could say the same of football. For the city-state mentality that still permeates Italian culture is pure football experience.

Support your team, support your city – or at least your version of your city. And in Manchester, they have two versions.

'Listen, Rob, it's just an accident of birth, you don't have to support City, you don't have to suffer for the rest of your life.'

Wilson and Gretton are in a Manchester pub before the game. Before a derby game. The background is simple. Rob is from south Manchester, Wythenshawe, as we said, the mother of all council estates. Wilson is from Cross Lane corner, Salford. South Manchester means you support Manchester City, unless you're really south, which is Cheshire, which means rich, which means you support United 'cause who – when they've got money – wears shit clothes and eats shit food?

And Salford is by the docks, just a walk down Trafford Road to Old Trafford, the home of Manchester United.

Before the Second World War they had both had turns at being big clubs in the English First Division. Their real pride should be in the radical work that their didn't-give-a-fuck players did for players' rights around the time of the First World War. It doesn't matter if you don't know about this, but you should probably read more.

But let's get past the war. For the second half of the twentieth century, there was only one big team in Manchester. Yeah, and we sell T-shirts in Malaysia by the bucketload, so fuck off.

United's global glory rests rightly on the twin peaks of tragedy and genius.

In the fifties, the Munich air crash – not just a football team dead, but a team of unarguably brilliant young players. Buddy Holly to the power of ten.

And then the sixties, Best-Law-Charlton. The inclusion in one team of three players whose physical and mental abilities could thrill the soul. This was the other part of the dreaming image that was Manchester United.

'You could always move, Rob, change your birth certificate or something. It's just a tragic accident that you were born in the land of the losers. You really don't have to spend the rest of your life on the Kippax reliving some unpleasant experience you had in potty training. Move, lie low, come back supporting a great team.'

Wilson was only half taunting his partner. He may even have been trying to help.

Gretton remained quiet, unperturbed, used to this shit and knowing if he got involved he would probably have to punch this fucking wimp out, and since he hadn't knocked Wilson over for a couple of years now, since he put that shite Geordie band of crusties on as support for Joy Division at the Russel, he wasn't going to start now and soil his hands with this piece of United shite.

'Fuck off, To'. I'll see you Monday.' And finishing his pint, Gretton left Wilson to his Sambucca and headed off to join his City mates and march up Stretford Road with them surrounded by the usual mounted police escort. This derby was at the home of United.

In the scoreboard end, taken over for the afternoon by the losers in light blue, Gretton swayed and cheered and sang. His favourite tune of the moment was an elegant mantra that went by the title of 'Swales Out'. Performance of said tune required the constant repetition of 'Swales' and 'out'. The hidden reference was to Manchester City's mild-mannered, sweet and rather ineffective chairman, Peter Swales. As United put the first goal past Joe Corrigan, the City goalie, Gretton's performance became more vital and passionate.

He realized that his stirring efforts were being matched by a tall young lad standing a few feet from him, clearly someone else who believed in this club and felt deep and abiding anger at their chairman's lack of ambition. They smiled at each other; exchanged silent understandings.

Ninety minutes gone, a 2-0 defeat, and the knowledge that even if they'd won 2-0, those bastards in red would still be the bigger team, the bigger brand, the numero uno in this divided town. They waited the obligatory twenty minutes for the Greater Manchester police force to siphon away most of the home supporters and then let the paler-than-before blue throng out onto the streets, to be herded, protectively and contemptuously back into the city two miles away where, if they wanted to, they could wreck a public house or two.

Half a mile into this strategic retreat, Gretton and his new mate peeled off. Fuck the police and fuck protection. But barely had they got fifty yards down an Old Trafford side street than there ahead of them, a dozen or so reds came round the corner. Discretion, running like fuck, is indeed the better part of valour and the two blues took off like Bill Shankly had just given them his Saturday afternoon pill. Hell for leather that barely saw the pavement. The whooping pursuit was getting closer. It was their area, they knew the streets. Cracked ribs beckoned. They turned out of sight briefly, Gretton shouted, and jumped over a garden wall. The two escapees hid behind same wall as the pack chased past, and shouted their way into the distance.

'Hi, I'm Rob. Rob Gretton.'

'Alright. Mike, Mike Pickering.'

They had jumped into the Garden of Eden and they were not to be ejected. It was, and they were, well met.

38
THE ALL NIGHT PARTY STOPS

Rob introduced Mike to his partners and soon he was in. Booker at the Haçienda. Find some bands to fill this incredibly beautiful and incredibly empty space.

And it wasn't just the club that was loitering on the edge of dissolution. One of the Factory bands was growing awry.

Not Rob's lot. New Order were exploring and developing, 'Blue Monday' leading the way for British music to combine dance and rock in a way that had long existed in the heart of Mancs, hospitable to both forms and never knowing the difference, but which was now becoming contagious.

It was Wilson and Erasmus who had a problem with their artistes, A Certain Ratio. They had become musicians. Never a great idea.

The Haçienda was three-quarters empty. That is, there were three or four people hanging out. Ratio were on stage, Gretton, Erasmus, Wilson and Pickering were leaning at the bar.

Ratio were giving a tight rendition of their Latin percussion classic, 'Skipscada'.

The partners in their record company were not impressed.

'Are they playing what I think they're playing,' said Wilson.

'Jazz,' hissed Erasmus.

'They've betrayed us, we should have them shot,' said Gretton, matter-of-factly.

'Maybe it'll work. We've never had a jazz band,' suggested Erasmus, looking for a way forward.

Tony Wilson (Steve Coogan).   Alan Erasmus (Lennie James).

Rob Gretton (Paddy Considine).   Lindsay Wilson (Shirley Henderson).

Tony and Lindsay at the Sex Pistols gig...

... with Bernard Sumner (John Simm), Peter Hook (Ralf Little) and Rob Gretton.

Rob, Ian Curtis (Sean Harris), Tony and Lindsay at Palatine Road.

Andy Serkis as Martin Hannett.

Peter Kay as Don Tonay.

Joy Division mark two: Bernard, Ian, Peter, Stephen (Tim Horrocks).

A Certain Ratio.

New Order live.

Tony with Granada boss Charles (John Thompson).

Tony Wilson with the Happy Mondays.

The Mondays rehearse: Bez (Chris Coghill), Paul Ryder (Paul Popplewell), Shaun Ryder (Danny Cunningham).

Yvette (Kate McGowan), Tony and the Haçienda queue.

Inside the recreated Haçienda.

'Jazz,' said Wilson. 'Jazz is like theatre, it's what people do if they can't get a proper gig. It's one down from *Celebrity Squares*. Form over content, the only sliver of pleasure is from the melodies they steal from popular song, the twats. Like Zappa said, jazz isn't dead, it just smells funny. You can always tell jazz – the fuckers on stage are having more fun than the audience.'

'Bongos,' said Rob, angry now, 'they've got fucking bongos. Shooting is too good for them.'

'Wait on guys, remember the corporate claim: artistic freedom, we promised all our bands complete freedom. Freedom to fuck off and free-dom to play whatever they want to play,' said Wilson, stifling resentment and disappointment.

The others shuffled off to have a joint in the office, Wilson went to the dressing room to do his job of consoling the band for the low turnout and promised himself he would not go into the art criticism thing at this point.

The group were pissed off.

'Where is everybody? Are you unable to promote a bloody gig?' Simon, still the leader, still arrogant, though now he merely led his way through a set of timbales.

'It was great, don't worry. Remember the Sex Pistols gig. Well, you don't, but I do. How many people were at that?'

'Who gives a shit.'

'No, it's important. Probably forty people. And it was history.'

'But there were only thirty in tonight.'

'Exactly. The smaller the attendance, the bigger the history. There were only twelve people at the Last Supper, thirteen when it started, half a dozen at the *Kittyhawk*. Archimedes was on his own in the bath.'

Never say die, never give in, never lose the positive force. But the Archimedes one was taking it a bit far. Desperation setting in, encouraged by the jazz disdain.

Who was right, the partners or the band? Who can tell. A great girl called Sadie or something with fabulous backless dresses went on to do pretty bloody well with jazz. Bland it out a bit and sell it to the thirtysomethings to play at their dinner parties. But Factory wasn't CBS and Simon Topping was never going to wear backless dresses. Instead, he would go and do a course in piano tuning. Lost talent, misplaced genius, and maybe it was Wilson who misplaced it.

There's a strange fact of life about good second division bands. They're more arrogant than first division bands. First division bands know about music. Marketing, accountancy, design? Fuck off, that's what you guys do.

But the second division band, who seduce you with their real abilities to write fine songs, such fine songs, these fuckers know everything about everything. The world economy, distribution incentives, travel arrangements; they're the boys. They know everything. And everybody else knows shit.

And they die. Their careers bleeding die. It's a shame, but I'm not crying anymore.

39
WHAT ABOUT HEWAN CLARKE?

We have been going with the accepted version of history over the past few pages, all that stuff about the Hac being a disaster and being empty and being shit. Which is funny, 'cause I'm laughing and our heroes never saw a fucking penny back from the millions they all ditched in, but I must say something here for the record.

There were some great Saturday nights. Hewan, the DJ, played some good stuff, and just 'cause we all take the piss out of hairdressers doesn't mean we should diss the pre-Aceeeed audience. In fact, in the immortal words of another clever DJ, McCready, Hewan played the fuck out of Man Parrish to try and get under the hair of hairdressers and into their souls.

And twice a year, on New Year's Eve and the May birthday bash, there was no place on earth like the Haçienda. That's a fact. Stone cold fact.

Stand-out tune was Lulu's 'Shout' on those party nights, hardly hip but these were the days of the war (against all white New Romantic shite) and we did have rationing.

And although the plan had been to spend the money they made from Joy Division on this holy of holies and although they ended up spending everything they made from everything and then some, the Factory boys were happy. They took the monthly near-death bankruptcy meetings with stoical good grace. And they had done what they intended to do. Built Manchester a piece of New York that steamed with civic pride, their civic pride. Reinvestment was the eighth virtue, pride no longer a sin.

It became a mantra to rubbish the Scousers, the scallies down the road with their backs to the Irish Sea. They had created the modern world as we know it. The Beatles and their Merseybeat cohorts had wrapped the globe in the glories of popular culture, fulfilled the prophetic hip grind of E. Presley and rescued the youth-of-then world from Bobby Darin.

And where was their city now, where was Liverpool? On its arse, with Gizzzza Job as its strap-line. And why? 'Cause the lovable moptops had deserted their city the first bloody minute they could afford the train fare and fucked off to that shithole London. Where did they invest their money, where did they build their empire? Apple was in Saville Row. Saville bloody Row. Arseholes. Apple bloody core.

Why had those early Factory releases had that magical Hannett sound? The young genius had been able to plug his digital thingy into the outboard racks of a major world-class thirty-six-track studio that was in Stockport – Stockport, ladies and gentlemen, Stockport, because 10CC were a Manchester band and they had taken the proceeds of the delicious 'I'm Not in Love' and had reinvested in their home. Reinvested. Built a fuck-off studio. Respect. (Sorry about that 'Don't Like Cricket' song, but otherwise, massive respect.)

And Liverpool in the early eighties? Like the Cavern and Northern Songs had never happened.

To be fair and principled here, and not wanting to shit on the Scousers too much, the bastards do have an excuse. They're Irish.

Apparently, unscrupulous Liverpool traders in the nineteenth century, having made their bit out of the slave trade, got a second whack out of the emigration business. They had ships to take people to America; all they had to do was unscrew the shackles. Easy.

But wait, the potato famine; those Irish buggers want to get to America too. So they invented the first two-stop strategy. In Dublin and Cork, fill the boats. Sail to Liverpool. Tell them it was New York, and what the fuck did they know, and your man disembarked, happy in his new home and the boyos restocked the ships with the second house from the mainland.

Which is why Liverpool is Irish and since the dogma of diaspora is sacred to Irish culture, enshrined in the myth of the wild geese, we have to give them the right to fuck off. Even to London... which they did.

By the way, if you're thinking that one Manc band also fucked off to London and failed miserably to invest in their town, you'd be right. You'd be right, and they'd be Irish.

So screw the Scousers, but Mancs believe in their city. By and large, they stay, and they put stuff back in. And that was the Haçienda and that was why, despite the financial shite, the boys never stopped smiling.

And they thought they were alone, just them, the precious few, believing in their holy city. As years rolled on into the late eighties, they found out with pleasure, not irritation, that they had never been alone. The disease was widespread, though undiagnosed. Turned out other Mancs were at the renascence stage of their lives too. City councillors and city businessman, buying old warehouses, planning new lives for their town, dreaming of city reborn. The boys with the stupid club were mad, but not alone.

40

IT HAS THREE LETTERS, BEGINS WITH B AND ENDS WITH Z AND IN THE MIDDLE IS AN E

There now follow two unlikely but symbolically accurate events. The first begins in outer space, or Little Hulton, which is to say, a place where the atmosphere is rarefied and survival tough.

Little Hulton is outer space, the space on the outer limits of Salford. First you have Salford, the working-class city that does a Minneapolis-St Paul with big brother Manchester. The languid, bendy and generally filthy River Irwell holds the worked-in city and the lived-in city apart. But only just. And beyond Salford you get the suburbs of Salford, the Eccles and the Swintons. No longer the soap-opera side streets, but clearly connected. Then there's Worsley, a polite, middle-class enclave with some half-timbered crap that reminds us that Salford is multidimensional, but then go further out, go further out into space, and we have Little Hulton. Not the back of beyond but the beyond of the back. Almost on the East Lancs Road, the classic 50s dual carriageway that connected the warring twins that were Liverpool and Manchester; Little Hulton, a place that was simply, 'on the way out'.

And there, one day, we see a sixteen-year-old Shaun Ryder walking down the middle of the street, 'cause he's off pavements today. He's off school too. In trouble 'cause his teachers say he cheated in a poetry competition. Not that his school is big on poetry, but they do try occasionally, and when young Mr Trouble handed in his it was clear from the strangely moving language and rhythms that Mr and Mrs Ryder needed to come in to school to be berated for their son, who had evidently moved on from stealing stereos and televisions to stealing literature.

Of course, Shaun had written it. Of all the lies told in this book, this is the one that isn't. He could write. His school didn't know it and the cool thing is, he didn't know it. Still doesn't.

He'd been barred for the day. Education is so uneducated. And now, wandering aimlessly of an eleven o'clock morning, he heard a whoosh, a swoosh, a roar, and the estate tarmac began to tremble.

A flying saucer, approximately two hundred yards wide, hovered at the far end of the cul-de-sac. Hovered, but swayed a bit too. Side to side. Fairly rhythmic. The outside was all matt silver, that finish you get from Humbrol acrylic on Airfix plastic in an imaginary world sort of way. And where you would expect to see the numbers inscribed by a Starfleet stencil, instead three large bronze letters in perfect Helvetica type. B, E and Z.

For one second the saucer stopped its baggy dancing, and then a great clap of thunder like God farting and a flash of white neon filled all of Shaun's senses. And whooooooo the saucer reappeared in vision just long enough to shake its corners at young Ryder and retreat at a million miles a second into the furthest point of the sky.

And as sense and sensibility returned to our lad, he saw, twenty or so yards away, in the aura that the alien ship had left behind, another lad. Taller than himself, but of a similar age and with an angular look, eyes perching forward like those of a bird of prey, looking for stuff. Searching for stuff.

'Fly me to the moon,' says Ryder and hummed the Truffaut signature tune from *Close Encounters*. 'Do da do deee doooo.'

It is an alien. 'Do da da dooo deeeee dooo. Thunderbirds are go, buddy, going to the foot of our stairs.'

'Put those words back into my mouth, you thieving bastard.' Shaun grins broadly. They both sway. Walk together. Embrace. Connect. Walk away from the cul-de-sac, together. Grinning. Grinning.

41
A LOADED GUN

That same day, back on Palatine Road in south Manchester, Alan and Tony are hanging out trying to do some company accounts. Not going well, so they have another number for the road. And the road goes nowhere. Normal. The flat bell rings. Erasmus reminds Wilson of the company rule. If it's anyone asking for Erasmus he's not there, and the most anybody knows is that he left for the Soviet Union seven months ago and hasn't been since. Parking fines, alimony, stuff like that. To live outside the law you must be brutally honest, except when it's a bailiff at the door.

Wilson goes into the corridor, past the cardboard box where they throw the demo tapes. There is a single line pencil drawing of a man with his arms out on the wall above the box. The stick man is labelled in sprawling capitals, 'Mike Pikering', 'cause he's now the Factory A&R man. The box is full of tapes. It's emptied once a fortnight into the outside bin. Fuck demo tapes.

And fuck this doorbell, alright, alright.

Door opens.

Surprise.

'Hello, Martin,' says Wilson, with a warmth and an inquisitive twist. His face lights up. 'Great to see you.'

Martin smiles too. Raises his right hand, which contains a gun, points it straight at Wilson, that 'one-way fucking mirror that was the chairman of the board' in Martin's own tender words, and pulls the trigger twice.

Three bangs, two the gun, the third Wilson hitting the deck fairly bloody hard.

Hannett, still smiling, turns back onto the landing and walks at even pace down the stairs.

Wilson, quickly aware that there is no blood, and no pain, but humiliation and a cracked right hip, says to the retreating back of his ex-partner and smack-drenched genius, 'Thanks, Martin.'

After all, it was another experience, wasn't it?

You may be asking, 'Did these events really happen? Sounds like something out of a movie.'

Shooting his old mate. With blanks. When would Martin use blanks?

Facts, please.

On the occasions when he would phone Rob and engage New Order's manager in conversation – and remember, it was the fact that Gretton, Wilson and Erasmus let their musicians move on from Martin's tutelage that had really hurt; lovers always have to choose, and when his partners chose their musicians, the death wish for them set in – and when the phone call with Rob was going nowhere, Martin had simply pointed a gun at the receiving end of the phone handset and blown it away. Twice. Real bullets. Reality. Sufficiently disconcerting that Rob had to get one of his lawyers to issue restraining orders. You will be restrained from blowing away phones that I am on the other end of, you fucker.

And the other bit, Martin and Tony, the imaginary visit by the ex-partner. Well, Martin did come to the door, but it wasn't the office and it wasn't the morning... A couple of times, in fact, he turned up at Wilson's house in Old Broadway. Late on rainy nights. Wilson opened the door. Hannett just stood there. Crying silently. In the rain. Like a line from a Willie Nelson song, and as deeply sad as Nelson's voice. There was no animosity, just distance and nostalgia between them now. The lawsuits and litigation two or three years gone. The thirty-five grand settlement also long gone, into Martin's primary nervous system.

Wilson would invite his ex-partner in. They talked, or he talked. Martin talked about Ian. And cried some more. A conversation that was rambling and tear-stained. Wilson was embarrassed. Embarrassed that he had been able to get on with it, get on with life and all the stuff that filled time and thought. And Martin hadn't. He hadn't got over the brutality of that Saturday night and Sunday morning in Macclesfield. Why and what and how were still Martin's main line of enquiry. Wilson felt shallow. Hannett felt pain. And maybe, if the drugs let him, he also felt the little rivulets that periodically stung his cheeks. At midnight, Hannett went back out on to the street. No plans to talk or see each other again. No explanation of the visit. It had happened. It would happen again.

And the spaceship? True, of course. How else do you explain the onset of the Happy Mondays...

42
LOOSE FIT

Phil Saxe was a south Manchester Jewish boy, which is good news 'cause it meant he didn't make a big deal about it. North Manchester and you might as well carry the Wailing Wall on your fucking back. But south Manchester, Reform or not, was Jewish cool.

Musical lad, our Phil, hanging out at Wigan Casino and the like, not for the sulphate but for the irresistible drive of those soul classics that history would declare as Northern Soul 'cause the only fuckers that got these divine American sounds of the seventies were boys and girls from northern England who would dance like there was no tomorrow on the crest of honest chemicals and honest emotions.

Phil DJ'd at the Casino and other hotbeds. He was there and did it, but when it came to making a living, he would do as his tribe did. Not just buying and selling, he worked for a while as marketing boss at a frozen food company on the east coast, but come this decisive moment in his life, he was back in dear old Manchester and running a jeans stall on the Arndale Market.

I don't know who Arndale was or is. No one in Britain does. This is intelligent, since if we knew who the bugger was we'd all go round his house and drop some shit on his doorstep the way he did for the rest of us.

Sometime in the sixties, while John Lennon was telling the Maharishi to piss off and George Best was scoring goals direct from corner kicks, while everywhere the world was getting better, Mr Arndale was building shopping centres in British towns and cities. Shitting on our doorsteps.

Town centres, the thing called the High Street, were replaced by shopping malls. Now don't get me wrong, I like a good mall. The Beverly

Centre will do me any day, with its funky little pet shop at the car park entrance and an extremely good Banana Republic. And as long as I don't have to fly the much over-estimated Singapore Airlines – I'll take a week at Raffles any day – Singapore, the up-market shopping mall as city state is as good as the late twentieth-century got. Retail is of course short for relationship and we all like relationships.

But Arndale centres... The concourses were from the architecture of cruelty school. Let's revisit the situationist concept of drifting, the analysis of how streets and crossroads and vistas lead the human forward in an involuntary dream of spatial desire. You don't drift in an Arndale. You root and you die.

And if the insides were crass, specializing in lowest-common-denominator shops, the outsides were the pièce de résistance. As if a whole bunch of people had got together and said to themselves, 'Let's do ugly.'

And since these centres were meant to provide everything you might want inside, they were big, and the simple law of physics tells you that the outside was even bigger. Usually this was some red-brick monstrosity, but in the case of Manchester's Arndale, they went for tiles. White tiles that got dirty damn quick. If people are going to call it a toilet, let's give them a bit of a helping hand.

Years later, the IRA bombed the Manchester Arndale. A bleeding outrage. We'd wanted to bomb it for years and somebody beat us to it. The shame. Though we used the tragedy to wangle sizable cash-flow out of the government. Which was nice. And Phil's stall was nice, for all the exterior being crap.

One side of the Arndale was the big shops, British Home Stores and Bugs Bunny land. But the other was a basement that contained a market. For centuries, British towns have had their markets, covered stalls erected in the market square on a particular day of the week.

The Arndale market was on all week, and though buried underground 'cause the poor people who used the markets were obviously of the mole-like burrowing kind, it had a feel to it. The feeling of trade, of vending, of stuff.

And Phil had lots of stuff, lots of denim stuff.

How a French town managed to corner the market in Gold Rush outer-wear and then trend it on to leg coverings for men who never grow old is fascinating, but probably not part of this story. Except that Phil was a jeans man *par excellence*. Knew the sizes that were coming in, the cuts, the little details.

Only ever made one mistake.

In the late seventies, one of his suppliers told him he had a couple of hundred special outsized jeans with massive wide thigh room and 22-inch flares at the bottom. Been ordered for a Mongolian tribal reunion or something and were never picked up. Phil could have them at a quid a throw. Now, Phil didn't see this as a real soon-comer, but when the price came down to 50p, well, what could he say?

One hundred and ninety-five prime samples lingered in the storeroom. Five stellar examples of this equivalent of the wide-bodied jet remained tucked in a part of his stall. They were waiting. Phil was waiting. It was as if there was a Second Coming trip going on. The jeans and the Jew were waiting. But for what? It begins with the letter M. And we're wait-ing for what?

The year 1985 is what. Nineteen eighty-fucking-five, shortly after a UFO with the call sign BEZ was seen fucking off down the A580 at stel-lar knots.

'Oi, mate, what are these?'

Shaun Ryder and his younger brother Paul were doing the Arndale. Shopping, lifting, drifting.

'Ey?'

Phil didn't jump. It might be nothing.

'Some old stock. Very trendy, boys, very nice stuff.'

'You could get some action in these, man. Hey, our kid, check these.'

Shaun holds a pair against his brother's waist.

'What is it, man? Twenty-three?'

'Twenty-two,' said Phil, 'twenty-two inches.'

'I'm going to need five of them, for my band.'

Phil had held himself back. Had not wanted to believe too much, had not wanted to be disappointed too much. But now it was done. He looked at the elder Ryder, right in the eyes.

'It's you, isn't it?'

'Aye, it's me alright.'

The baggy Messiah.

43
A FAMILY AFFAIR

Phil wanted to see this group that belonged to his long-awaited denim saviour. Wanted to see them badly. Arranged to attend a rehearsal in a school room, after hours, in Swinton, the legislative capital of Salford and half a mile up the road and up the environmental scale from Little Hulton.

Shaun Ryder's band. In fact, Shaun Ryder's gang, and how many great groups have as their social structure the teenage gang? You can't do any better.

Brother Paul was on bass. Gary Whelan drummed and was handsome and PD played keyboards through a personality haze. Some say PD's otherworldliness came from walking into a pub in Swinton in 1983 and shouting something rude about Swinton sucking dick or something. He got a kicking that left part of his brain, clearly an important part, on the pavement. Others say it was the cautious nature of Ryder's gang who, whenever they discovered a new pill, liquid or potentially narcotic substance, would try it out first on PD to check the side-effects. Whatever had happened, PD performed hypnotic keyboards in a manner that implied he was personally and continually hypnotized.

The odd one out in the group was Moose, the guitarist. He was odd, and he was the odd one out 'cause he was kinda nice and the rest would have a go at him 'cause nice wasn't it.

It is by a deeply Dylanesque twist of fate that this seminally working-class band, whose very name celebrates the dole-queue celebrations of the lumpenproletariat, who hated getting out of bed, should ascend the sticky rungs of the music industry ladder courtesy of one of Manchester's most resoundingly dull middle-class suburbs. Bramhall is where Stockport meets

Cheshire, in that it doesn't even have the nerve to be boorishly rich, merely boringly rich.

Philip Saxe and Michael Pickering were residents of Bramhall, which merely proves that human beings have little control over where they are born and bred and must rise above these potential handicaps. Philip confided in Mike that he 'had' a band and they were good. Pickering arranged a support gig at the Haçienda for his mates to check out the Saxe recommendation. This was not a frequent activity. The fact that it was done at all implied the Pickering imprimatur and in the manner of all things with this lot, it would have taken something pretty shitty for the guys to have told the Pick to fuck off. As it was, the shambling bunch of scallies who sashayed out on to the dark shelf that was the Hac stage did more than enough. They had exactly what was being looked for. They had something and it was something that gave away absolutely no idea of what it was.

'They're cool. They've got something and I have absolutely no idea what it is,' said Wilson, leaning on the South African granite top of the Kim Philby Bar.

Gretton harrumphed. The Mondays were in. No one really knew why and that was, of course, exactly why.

Although, there were propitious signs. In the middle of the third number the lead singer seemed to be getting a little agitated with the rest of the band. In the manner of the famous Danish goalkeeper Schmeichel explaining to his back four that they were little better than worthless shit and that a slow death was too good for them, Shaun explained to his band that they were going 'too fucking slow'.

There was a lack of agreement from the assembled party, in particular the group's bass player, who could be lip-read as replying, 'Fuck off, you scaggy twat.'

Ryder elder then took a swing at Ryder junior, a scuffle commenced mid-stage and the group's monitor man came on from the side to sort it. Pushing in-between, he got his arms caught and all three went down in a sprawling, scrapping, rolling human lump. The rest of the band looked on with that seen-it-all-before stare and hey, whaddya know, the whole thing went up about 5 bpm. The bodies rolled and rolled and rolled, occasionally knocking into the drum riser and heading back to front of stage.

Saxe turned, worried about impressions, to the boys at the bar.

'It's OK, it's family, just family. Their dad Derek does the sound, that's him in there with them. Just family.'

'One child grows up...' muttered one of the board of directors. 'Cool,' said another.

Order restored and bpms upped, they got to the sixth number and Shaun was shouting again; not at the band, but at the audience this time. Screaming.

'Bez. Bez. Get up here.' The rest of the band were bemused, unamused. Their boss wanted his new mate from space on stage with them. Why?

'Bez, fucking get on stage.'

Out of the tide of humanity came the alien, a little embarrassed but with a wide grin and wide legs, gat-leggit, like Ursula Andress wading up the beach into all our lives and onto the Happy Mondays' stage.

'Dance, you fucker, and shake those maracas,' said the boss to an alien who was indeed already well maracca'd. And he started to move. Fuck, did he move.

Arms outstretched, slow wings feeling for the air in undulating fashion, hallucinogenic t'ai chi. And the shoulders, pressing forward beyond the alien's centre of gravity, always the shoulders.

And the audience, swaying and wondering what they were watching, found out what they were watching in watching Bez. Rock as dance, dance as rock. Bez.

It was the dance he'd brought back from his package trips to Ibiza and there were other things he'd brought back from Pink Floyd's island of More. Pupils the size of that thing that scores you seven points on a snooker table.

And later, when they made their way down the back stairs to the basement dressing room where half of the Whitworth Street drains seep down the back of three supersize Belfast sinks, they got a further taste of 'the family'. Guest list? What a fucking crowd. This is the group who in the years to come would take a fully spec'd colour photocopier to Glastonbury to knock out snide Triple A backstage passes for their personal guest list of 450.

Back then it was just eighty-odd, mostly still looking scally in that working-class football hooligan Fila Lacoste style, except that the lineaments of aggro had been replaced by the lineaments of MDMA, pure warmth in every fucking smile.

'This is me cousins, Mat and Pat and Karen. Our kids do the artwork for us.'

'Alright.'

Oh yes, very alright.

'Here, T, have one of these. Just come in from the Dam, best fucking quality.'

Wilson had heard that this new/old drug had been turning up over the past few weeks and fuelling the Haçienda's Friday night, where Pickering and his mates had been playing some obscure 12-inches that had seeped out of Detroit and Chicago.

In the corner of the dressing room, one of the Mondays' roadies was getting commercial and money was changing hands.

'Er, not tonight, thanks, stops me coming.'

Trying to impress his new kids, Wilson had delivered a little explicit intimacy and successfully, he hoped, inferred that as a man in the music business, he had drugs covered.

The old farts had indeed been there, done that. It was playing Texas in the early eighties. Backstage for any English band and the Blue Monday lot in particular, it wasn't sex that got offered but these little pills that were still legal in the Lone Star state. 'Cause who can be lone on this little love drug? Texas, so much to answer for. Doesn't sound as good, but it's the fucking truth.

And now it was the Dam. No names. Car trips. Import and no export. What was a Mondays roadie to do but feed this new market?

44
STELLA, QUID A PINT

Over the next few months, Factory's new band and a select group of DJs – Jon Dasilva, Graeme Park and the Pick – proceeded to piss petrol on this little bonfire.

Friday nights were for the super-cult who got the stripped-down beats of Aceeed emanating from mainly gay, black DJs in Detroit. America, in the throes of Aids-panic, ignored the spark cracked out of an obsession with gay dance that in its turn had its origins in the primitive synth experiments of Depeche Mode and New Order. That Basildon should have such a role in world cultural history is perhaps one footnote too many. That America should again ignore its black music roots, as it had done with the blues artists who meant so much to the first UK generation of beat groups, was just history repeating itself as farce.

It also managed to ignore its own little pill until mid-2001, when Oprah started showing pictures of the human brain before and after Ecstasy. Really? Does my head have holes in like that? Wow.

And truth be told, the drug that did the business was Stella Artois.

Friday nights were cool, which meant only four hundred or so punters. The Thursday afternoon management meetings debated the ensuing shortfalls. And the management was no longer the dumb-as-dogshit committee of the mid-eighties. Erasmus had kept telling Gretton and Wilson about some geezer called Paul Mason from Rock City, the successful Nottingham nightclub. He was studiously ignored until desperation set in and Erasmus got his way. It was tough for his partners. To admit they were wrong and Razzer was right was one thing, but to employ someone with long hair – urggghhh – who wanted to implement a student night – urggghhh – was hard to swallow.

And the student night made money. Fuck. The guy's alright. Needs a haircut, but he's alright. And Hooky rewarded him by arranging a Delta Integrale as Mason's company car. Hooky and cars was like Elvis with trucks, very endearing and more than generous.

As to sorting the Fridays, Mason suggested a cheap drink deal with their brewery, Whitbreads. There was a special offer on Stella, the reassuringly expensive lager.

Footnote 1:   Stella was the favourite urine-creator of the scallies.

Footnote 2:   In 1987, scallies were getting bored with being scallies.

If someone had said, 'Hey, the Ibiza bunch of football hooligans are particularly fond of Stella, let's make it a quid a pint, get them in the club, expose them to this new music, which is perfect for their summer holiday Manumission-style dionysiac dance that is let down by this Balearic beats crap – how can you dance to Cyndi Lauper when the Winter is upon you, DJ Oakenfold had explained to Wilson – and then we'll let the Mondays' crew sell them the marriage therapy drug round the back of our club and then we'll change the world,' they would have been fucking clever and it was never like that.

No one was clever. They couldn't spell serendipity, but you've got a dictionary somewhere, so look it up.

45
THE I.A. RICHARDS SCHOOL OF LITERARY CRITICISM

And something else was going on. The Factory boys enjoyed their new band, but had little handle on what it was they enjoyed so much. One day in his car, Wilson was listening to the next set of Mondays demos when a particular line broke his concentration. 'And Jesus was a cunt who never helped you with anything you did – or dunt.'

What is rhyme, what does it do and not do, what is it about the sense of words when scored to a sound pattern like that? Does something. And Ryder was doing something with his lyrics. Wilson began to be amazed at the way Ryder took a line to what seemed like an end and then hit a late and final note that completed all, that had all the dumb simplicity of Neil Young at his finest, but which in this case underscored the best piece of cynical atheism since Christopher Marlowe claimed that the Holy Ghost had beaten St Joseph to it.

Wilson got excited. Listened to more. On came 'Tart, Tart'.

He listened, rewound, listened, rewound, listened, rewound.

Je-e-e-sus.

First, the structure, three self-contained, sixteen-line stanzas. No chorus, just three perfectly complete short stories, three characters described; contained completely in three brief and extraordinary short stories. He never got clear who Maggot was, but the woman who was worried about 'the test on the blood' was a ravaged-looking middle-aged woman who hung around the Haçienda and even donated the club a pretty appalling painting. She dealt smack. She made the song.

But the first verse. 'When he came out of the lock-up, he said I'm looking for something better.'

Je-e-e-sus, it was Hannett, it was Martin.

Ryder did it again, the late close to a line. 'With his hand held out... Palms up.'

Where did last that fucking detail come from, why does it make the line explode?

Wilson rang Phil.

'That opening verse of "Tart, Tart", it's about Hannett, it is Hannett. I didn't know Shaun knew Martin.'

'He doesn't.'

'What do you mean, he doesn't?'

'He doesn't. Apparently he's been hanging out in Acid Corner at the Hac with Barney and listening to Barney's stories about Martin. Why?'

'Phil, your boy is the greatest lyric writer since Dylan and that includes that fucking Scouse misanthrope, Lennon. He's fucking genius.'

'Yeah. So what.'

Yeah, so what. What? The campaign to have Ryder made poet laureate was to be greeted by cries of 'What?' for years to come.

46
WACKA WACKA

The guys let the Pick have a work-out with the Mondays on their first single. OK, but no cigar.

Then Phil drafted in Vini. Wilson and Erasmus's guitarist was serenely driving his own path through the world. Every year or so he'd record an album of devastating beauty, the guitar patterns echoing with delicate emotions, and then put in just enough singing – reedy, asthmatic vocals rendering reedy asthmatic lyrics – to defer his canonization. But he was a guitarist's guitarist and Phil thought it might work. In love with the concept of family collaboration, Wilson gladly agreed and drove Vini over to the sessions in Strawberry.

Two hours later. A phone call.

'Pick me up now, immediately.'

'Vini, what's wrong?'

'These people are disgusting; their manners, their habits, their behaviour. I refuse to spend one more hour in their company, however brilliant they are. This is awful. Get down here immediately.'

Fifteen minutes later, Wilson parked up in the Stockport sidestreet and opened the door to the anguished and unpleased Reilly.

'Don't worry, they won't even notice I've gone. I thought you and Alan were bad, but these people do more drugs than God.'

'I'm really sorry, Vin,' said Wilson, crawling to his artist for somehow getting dogshit on his shoes.

'And that guitarist, what do they call him, Moose, the most useless guitarist I've ever met, had absolutely no idea what he was doing.'

There was a pause.

'Which is particularly interesting, since what he is actually doing is the most wonderful, bizarre and creative guitar playing that I've heard for fifteen years.'

The separation of the artist and his art. Vini's final comments were a vindication and prophecy. A mellow warmth spread through Wilson's brain as he taxied his guitarist back to Didsbury.

Next suggestion for producer. Bernard.

It was the inner circle's secret. More than a secret – it was something that they never talked about it. The greatest Manchester producer of the eighties was one Bernard Sumner. No one talked about it 'cause he was already becoming a difficult, full-of-himself son-of-a-bitch – what fucking pop star isn't – 'I told you, no planes with under fifty seats, re-route me' – and talking openly of Bernard's other genius was therefore a no-no for the guys. But genius-producer #2 it was.

Check out the early techno classic by Section 25, 'Looking from a Hilltop', check out Marcel King's divine pop classic, 'Reach out for Love', check out 52nd Street's Wythenshawe pop funk or the late eighties classic by Bernard's own Electronic, 'Getting Away With It'.

Doesn't say Produced by Bernard Sumner anywhere. But it screams Bernard Sumner with every brilliantly synched melodic click of the new music machines. So don't tell him, but the bastard inherited the Hannet mantle. Quietly and oh so successfully.

And there they were back in Strawberry six weeks later and Wilson was trying to enthuse New Order's lead singer, comfortably perched at the centre of the mixing desk.

'The lyrics are really important, Bernard, really important, Shaun's writing is very special. Shaun, Shaun, give Bernard an example of your lyrics.'

'Ugghh.'

'Tell Bernard some of your lyrics.'

Shaun looked a little blank, then, with a smile, reeled off his latest creation.

'Good, good, good, good, good, good, double good.'

Pause.

'... good.'

Bernard nodded. Wilson scrambled onwards.

'And then there's the guitar, the wah-wah stuff that we didn't have on the first single. The wacka-wacka stuff.'

Wilson was pulling at the water trying to get to the surface, to the air, to breathe, to make sense. When the Mondays were going it on stage, Moose had his body angled down over his guitar and was hitting that thing that can only be described as wacka-wacka. Maybe thwacka-thwacka. It was the sound of blaxploitation. These noises were the punctuation marks for the macho moments of *Shaft* and *Superfly*. It was the sound of colour, of black and the early seventies Technicolor whose cheapness mirrored the ghetto locations; and then that wacka-wacka stuff. A Harlem heartbeat.

'It's black stuff, it's dance stuff, Bernard. I know they're a group, a rock group, but they're something else. There's something else there.'

If Bernard heard or understood or cared, you wouldn't know. He'd learnt a lot from Hannett, not least how to handle yourself around non-geniuses with ideas.

But of course he got it. His solution: just play it, just record it, it being what they did. There was no mixing or messing.

Genius producer? His trademark was the deft interweaving of computerized melodies into a seamless piece of pop-joy. And he threw all that out the window and just recorded the bastards, as for live.

The only answer. See, great producer.

The resultant single, 'Freaky Dancing', is the roughest introduction to modern soul music the world will ever get. But that's what it was. The new soul music and as rough as the kids who dared to dream it.

47
ENTER NATHAN AND VINTEUIL

Not that the single sold, or the one after that or the one after that, or the album that came next. Of course they didn't sell. And Wilson prided himself on knowing why. It was because they were great artists, that's why.

On reflection, this is a pretty good mental trick for keeping your spirits up. Not enough to quote Shakespeare or Yeats, Wilson now moved on to Proust. If you're going to be this tosser who gets a rep for sprinkling expletives with great lines from the literary canon, then you can't get any finer than linking the great unwashed of popular culture to the great unread of academic literature. Fuck the fact that it's the best book ever written, 'cause no one believes you 'cause no one ever got past those first eighty-two pages where's he's lying in bed waiting for his mum to kiss him good-night.

Wilson had, and let it be known that he had read Proust, especially that bit where young Marcel creeps up on a cottage window and watches some Sapphic rug-munching on the sofa while Monsieur Vinteuil plays his sonata on the keyboard.

'Don't you see,' Wilson would tell anyone too polite to tell him to shut the fuck up, 'he was a penniless nobody and nobody wanted his bloody sonata, like no one wants the Mondays now. Penniless and ignored. Then in volume seven, twenty years later, Marcel attends the salon of the year and watches from the back of the room while the Great Vinteuil, now a regular Elton John in turn-of-the-century Paris, performs his Great Sonata to a hushed and thankful audience, the same bloody sonata that no one would touch with a shit-coated bargepole, just like punk, just like the Mondays. Just like Radio One.'

Marcel muses on how great artworks work. How we're all creatures of habit and only like what we've seen before, what we've heard before. And how what a great artist does is of its very nature new and therefore how it will inevitably be despised and shat on.

And how that artist might think of avoiding this real pain by never releasing said work. 'Doesn't work,' says Monsieur Proust, 'because the stuff has to be out there, has to be in the world so it can change the world.'

'Do you know what Proust said about Beethoven's Late Quartets?' said the motormouth, trying to explain the Mondays to any poor bastard who was still being polite. 'He said that Beethoven's Late Quartets spent their first fifty years in the world creating an audience for Beethoven's Last Quartets. Yes? Yes?'

Fuck off.

But at least it helped him. The consolation of another philosophy. It made him think that one day it would happen.

And of course it did.

Phil Saxe saw the day coming. From a few months off, Philip saw the dam beginning to shake, the concrete walls of disdain for the band from Little Hulton starting to lose the odd brick. When the dam broke and the penny dropped in the collective consciousness of British youth, it was going to be a torrent, washing all their lives along in front of them. Phil didn't want to become flotsam. Phil wanted a real life, a family life. He announced his retirement as manager of the Mondays.

On one of those long, grey, easy nights in the front room of 86 Palatine Road, Erasmus and Wilson were discussing important matters.

'Did you know that broccoli was invented by Cubby Broccoli?' Wilson took another long drag on the joint.

'You what?'

'Honest, Al, Cubby Broccoli, the film producer, his family anyway, invented this new vegetable by crossing a... er...' This story had seemed easy when he started ten seconds ago, but was already getting difficult.

'Er... crossing a cauliflower, with err...' Smoke exhales. Silence.

'You're fucking joking.'

'No, honest, Al, I promise.'

'Are you telling me the Bond films were financed by a deformed vegetable?'

Wilson was still trying to think what the hell you would cross with a cauliflower to get those...

'Honest, Al.'

'Anyway,' said Erasmus, 'I was thinking about Phil going. Why not get Nathan to manage the Mondays?'

Masterstroke. Nathan 'Nabs' McGough was Factory's concession to geography. A Scouser, with the wit to become an honorary Manc. Sort of Oasis in reverse. He had done a post-modern Russel Club in Liverpool with a thing called Plato's Ballroom in Liverpool in the early eighties and then had got on board with the older Factory lads by managing one of Factory's mid-eighties cult sellers, Kalima. Remember them? Sade two years too early, progressive Latin American jazz from a Hulme squat. And he had been the coolest manager on the scene. A great manager takes on the aura of his band (in this case, progressive and with a chilled funk) and adds the businessman crap to wind people up. Nathan was good.

The mid-eighties had seen Nabs hike back up the M62 and handle some Liverpool outfit. All melody, no attitude probably, although having never seen them this is probably just blind prejudice on the part of your author. But around this time Nathan got a rep for handling difficult artists who had a drug thing. His technique was shrouded in mystery but it was claimed his knack was to take more drugs than his artists. Probably just a publicity line on his CV. But he was good, and Alan's idea was good.

48
I ASKED FOR LINES, BIG LINES

The day was getting on. Wilson took his car out of the Granada car park and crossed town to a basement disco on Princess Street, at the far end of Manchester's triumphal avenue lined with great six-storey mercantile monuments. This was the rougher end and had become handbag disco land. In just such a handbag, Nathan's video-makers, two Geordie Coppolas, were hard at work on the next Mondays video, for a song called 'Wrote For Luck'.

> I wrote for luck, they sent me you.
> I asked for lines, you formed a queue
> I asked for juice, you gave me poison...
> Is there anything else you can do...

Eat your heart out, Yeats. Does anyone out there get it yet? Do they? 'You used to speak the truth but now you're clever...' Awwww fuck it. Let's just get the video done.

That night, the Mondays crowd would dance and writhe on the tight Manhattan dance floor. They would be filmed mooching and moving and caressing the spaces between them, eighty or so boys and girls, mostly E'd to the nines and giving a defining visual moment to the Aquarian rush that would dawn a few months later. A vision of humanity as maggots in the fisherman's plastic sandwich box, mingling and wriggling, but now not disgusting, but sensuous, communal, hypnotic.

And in the afternoon, they'd shoot the alternate video. Schoolkids. Jesus, a load of schoolkids in their Sunday best, dancing on the same dance floor.

Sounds good. Two vids for the same song for the price of one. Why not?

Wilson walked into the space and saw Phil and Keith and their mate, the King of Super-8, circling the dancing kids with their camera while 'Matchstalk Men', that gruesome tribute to a man who did better paintings of the sea than he did of cotton mills in Stalybridge, bounced out of the sound system.

Brian and Michael; inoffensive names for such an offensive outing.

'Er, why are we doing this to this?' asked the man who has to sign the cheques. It's great being the guy who signs the cheques. Ask Harvey Weinstein. Just great. It means you can ask questions like, 'Er, why are we doing this to this?'

'Oh, that,' said Phil. 'It's the same bpm and we haven't got the track yet. It's meant to be coming later.'

'What, no track? But they've been in studio all week. What's the fucking problem?'

'Well, you know how long he can take when he's mixing a track.'

'When who's mixing a track?'

'Oh, I'm sorry, did no one tell you? It's Martin.'

'It's Martin?'

Dazed and a mite confused, Wilson bade the Baileys goodbye and good luck and headed off into the night, the car and the next chapter.

49
OLD MAN: FALL TO THY PRAYERS

'Hello Hannett, you wanker.'

It was safe to say that.

Hannett was in the live room tweaking Paul Ryder's bass and Wilson was behind one foot of strengthened glass in the control room.

Wilson hadn't done his apeshit routine. Why did no one tell me etc. As described by the Durutti Column's drummer, and the boss of Manchester's premier PA company, Bruce Mitchell, formerly of Greasy Bear – and if you don't remember who they were from the beginning of the book, then it's not my fault if you don't take things in – Bruce would describe his manager's outburst of petulance as rhino-coming-out-of-thicket mode, which was, as Bruce always is, utterly accurate, and carried the weight of the older and wiser man which Bruce always was.

This time the rhino stayed behind the thicket. Chewed on a few leaves. The idea of using Hannett for the next Mondays tracks was Alan's and Nathan's and was of course inspired. Wasn't this all about throwing genius into the bowl and whisking it all up together to see what the cake tastes like? And there was the empathy bit. Martin had the same affinity for mind alteration as the band. That is to say, total. Utter. And in particular, the brown. The dope boys like Tony and Alan were outsiders here.

'The thing you have to remember about heroin, if you think you'll be able to deal with it T, is that it's the most wonderful thing in the world. Understand that, believe that and then maybe you can handle it,' Martin once explained to his partner.

And Shaun had the Monkey too. When those film-makers in the year 2000 first tried to write about Shaun the script had more syringes scattered around than in the prop-room for *Trainspotting*. But that wasn't the way. Ever. Shaun chased the dragon. He chased the fucking dragon across five continents and damn nearly fucking caught it. That was Shaun.

The perfect producer, then, the empathetic genius. And Wilson wouldn't admit it, but the return of the friend, the return of the partner, was a result for all sides, a moral thing. Felt like warm sex. Great move.

'Wilson, you wanker.'

Hannett's response through the studio window was easy and immediate, the friendly contempt for the one-way mirror/chairman of the board was a simple continuum as if seven years had been erased in a second.

'What do you want, Wilson, you wanker?'

'I want the fucking record, you wanker. What's keeping you, run out of ideas?'

'I haven't run out of bullets if that's what you think.'

'So if I open this door, are you going to try and shoot me?'

'No, but I might give you a heart attack.'

Wilson pushed the heavy studio door ajar and thereupon had his heart attacked by the solemn image of a man who had put on ten, maybe fifteen, stone. It's the problem with smack. Get off it and you probably go on the beer. You're still a soul that's been bought and sold, but now you're also fat, boring and usually smell a bit.

Martin would later play a bit part in a video for one of his last, non-Factory, bands, the New Fads. He was wheeled around the set, which, with an irony he was too far gone to enjoy, happened to be the dancefloor of the Haçienda, in a supermarket trolley. A great barrel of flesh, half in, half out of a Tesco tram, head lolling, insensate. Every word that Shakespeare wrote about Falstaff in Henry IV parts one and two and Act One of Henry V is contained and fully imaged in that ten seconds of tragedy and farce that was the trolleying of the man who changed drum sounds forever.

Martin waved the brandy bottle in Wilson's direction.

'Great band, though, Wilson.'

50
WALKING THROUGH VINYL

So Martin and the Mondays hit it off. The man whose stories Shaun had memorized was now their new guru. For a while. For now. And it was to be a trip.

For the main album session they moved into Driffield.

Where?

Exactly. Near Hull. North of Hull. Somewhere. Yorkshire, but who the fuck knows or cares. A market town where some intelligent teen pop outfit of the mid-eighties had constructed a recording studio around an old coach house on the High Street.

Take the M62 across the moors and then go on for hundreds of miles and get off at Junction 27. Head north-north-east for thirty more miles. Driffield.

He'd been told they'd be in the pub on the High Street. Wilson wandered in around nine o'clock. Almost empty. No Mondays, but there were signs that they had been there. There were two squaddies at a table in the corner of the pub's front room. Young soldiers from the nearby army camp; Driffield was an army town. The boys in brown were staring at glasses of Coca Cola. And they were smiling gently, very gently. You can't sell coals to Newcastle, but you can sell E to members of Her Majesty's armed forces. The Mondays were obviously a hit in Driffield.

Wilson moved down the street, passing some equally off-it squaddies who were out for the night (and smiling) and turned into the courtyard of the studio complex. Waved in by the guy in the front office, he crossed to the control room and stepped inside. Hannett and Gary Whelan, the handsome-as-hell drummer, were intent on the mixing desk. Knobs, lots of knobs.

'Hi, guys, it's just me.'

They didn't turn or look for a second, then Martin began to swing on the swinging chair and pull his arm up from under his jumper like he was bringing out a... And he pointed the gun at Wilson, only it was two fingers in a traditional British 'V' and he laughed as Wilson caught his involuntary lurch before it got truly embarrassing.

'Now then, Martin, none of that. You're a big lad, but you're out of condition and you can't hurt me. You could sit on me, but you couldn't hurt me.'

Fat jokes were not part of Martin's universe, so he just suggested that Wilson fuck off to the band rec room across the courtyard and let the men get on with the work.

Wilson traipsed off to the directed band rec room. Every studio has one. They are inhabited always by pool tables and boredom. Join the navy and see the world. Join the music industry and see pool tables. And boredom.

But the glass door to the band room was papered over and there seemed to be no lights on inside; a heavy thump, thump was coming from the walls. The courtyard was dark, the room as Wilson opened the door even darker. Thump, thump, thump. Great noise. Wilson picked his way across a floor that was strewn with 12-inch circles of black vinyl, half in, half out of their sleeves, and stumbled over the legs and bodies of maybe ten people. Thump, thump.

'Alright T, how's it going?'

'Alright, alright.'

It was a Tuesday night in Driffield. The Mondays were having a party. As Wilson picked his way through the room he tiptoed through his favourite metaphor. Cultures coming together, streams merging into rivers. All that shit.

No more words, he was wading through it. The vinyl floor coverings were the latest imports from Chicago and Detroit. This was the finest stuff. House before some fucker decorated it. Maybe Pickering, Park and Dasilva played these tunes last Friday night at the Hac. Maybe Pickering, Park and Dasilva would play them next Friday night at the Hac. The virus wasn't being spread. It was being ingested and absorbed and gobbled up.

Influences. Three cheers for 'influences'.

51
IT'S A CLASS THING

The album that emerged from Driffield was *Bummed*; it flopped. Everyone thought the group was just too scummy or something. Too working class or something. Funny thing about rock and roll, it likes to think it's working class. Don't know why. And mostly it isn't. The Beatles went to fucking grammar school, and why Lennon's accent was rougher in '65 than it was in '60 is just a straightforward rock-and-roll thing.

Punk? Alright, John Lydon, you were working class and you can stop shouting about it 'cause I'll do right by you even if you don't do right by me, but by and large it was a fucking art-school mafia put-up job, and Strummer was a fucking diplomat's son. So mostly it's middle class and we like to avoid that damaging item of truth.

But Elvis was working class. White-pantie man was real. And this generation that was about to explode out of Ibiza package holidays into the wet dreams of every marketing man in Europe. They came from the non-property-owning classes. It's important. It explains the start and it explains the finish. And it explains why no one would take Wilson's grandiose claims for the Mondays seriously.

And Wilson's claims were getting grander by the minute. He was now talking about T.S. Eliot. Not that Shaun's verbal style had any connection. That was Ian. It had been obvious to Wilson from early on that the Curtis style had the clipped, tight rhythms and even the starkness of vocabulary of a T.S. Eliot. And references to Gaultier (not Jean-Paul, thank you) and Romanticism in some T.S. Eliot reference book that he had skimmed and failed to remember haunted the back regions of his brain when it came to thinking about Ian's poetry. Romanticism?

But Shaun Ryder. Yeats, OK, but where could we connect the post-secondary-modern intellect of this northern drug aficionado with the bank clerk stiffness of Thomas Stearns Eliot?

Ask Neil Tennant. Long before the Pet Shop Boy had given Factory a cool-as-fuck hit with him and Barney and Johnny Marr, that piece of perfection mentioned in praise of Bernard, 'Getting Away With It', Neil and his mate had invaded the world with 'West End Girls', which he himself is happy to confess owes much to *The Waste Land*, reflecting the idea of a singular poem in many voices. Thank you, Neil.

Ask Shaun Ryder and he wouldn't know or care what you were talking about. And yet, even more than 'West End Girls', the next Mondays release, the classic 'Lazyitis', reflects exactly the *Waste Land* aesthetic. For in *The Waste Land*, Eliot not only uses voices, but segues from quote to quote, from stolen scene to stolen scene, from a piece of Wagner to the Upanishads, from a Middleton Revenge Tragedy to Chaucer's opening of the *Canterbury Tales*. Each theft explodes the mood of the stolen-from piece and enriches the base with all of it.

And Shaun photograph-me-with-the-kind-of-topless-glamour-models-who-give-porn-a bad-name Ryder? He could do that. Oh, he could do that.

'Lazyitis' begins as a memory of maternal satire. The elegant Mrs Ryder would regularly tell her son he had lazyitis. It's a northern thing. Adding 'itis' to the chosen adjective.

Perfect text for a song. But Ryder starts to weave in the attachments, the enrichments. For starters he puts his mum's loving put-down into the form of that favourite children's physical rhyme – you know, the one where your mum and dad tickle each toe in turn until the final little piggy goes whee whee whee all the way home. Well, the first toe has lazyitis, and you can figure out the rest.

Brilliant, but that's just for starters.

Then, since it's a mother and son reunion, why not do the Eliot bit by opening with the greatest of all songs about family? Sly Stone's great musings on family relationships, the story of the good brother and the 'bad' brother, actually opens the song. Just like T.S. Eliot, it brings in all the warmth of the original and factors in everything the listener ever felt about 'Family Affair'.

Not enough, not enough.

Suddenly, you're into a Beatles tune, and while talking about an ache that makes him ache qualifies for a coupla stars, the fact that this whole section bit is a direct melodic reference to The Beatles' early pop period is stunning. Combining Beatles purity with some seeming syphilis or cold turkey stuff. Yoking of opposites, weird and extremely successful in literary terms.

And that was 'Lazyitis', first time round. But there was more. The Mondays' film-makers, the aforementioned Geordie couple who called themselves the Bailey Brothers, were working on a Hand movie.

If you know who the Bailey Brothers were – the Bailey Brothers Mortgage and Loan company, that is – that's good. If you don't, it's OK but you should probably watch Christmas TV movies more.

And a Hand movie is exactly that. A Hand movie. The central character is a severed hand that does things – you know what I mean. Anyway, this was called 'The Revenge of the One-Armed Boxer' and the Baileys wanted to use an elderly gentleman they had come across in a northern cabaret club for the part of the boxer's trainer. That was Karl Denver, a Country and Western-type Lancashire lad, who back in the sixties had had a massive hit with 'Wimoweh'. Yes. 'Wimoweh'. Fucking classic.

A friendship had grown up with the gentleman from Reddish. And when the Mondays met him he was invited to come in and add some voices to a new recording of 'Lazyitis'.

New voice, let's have a new bit. Wilson, already smarting from the sheer accounting complexity – and accounting was complex for the Factory crowd – of reporting royalties to Sly Stone and The Beatles' publishers (Michael Jackson, do I really have to pay you, haven't you got enough?) was astonished on arriving at Strawberry to find that Ryder had inserted a whole new section.

Hello, David Essex.

Now the centre and end of the song were wrapped in the trite but immortal 'We're Going To Make You A Star'.

Bloody hell.

And stirring it all together, Hannett gave it the final kiss of creative genius by ending the song with a 'round', that traditional old English folk structure, where somebody starts a chorus and then another starts on the first line when the first guy starts the second and so on and round and round. That's why they call it a...

Karl and Shaun's voices entwine like two rose trees planted in the corpses of lovers. Shaun does Sly, Karl does Beatles. Shaun does ooooooohh. Shaun does a thing with his lips, clicking. Karl does Mrs Ryder, Shaun does David Essex. And then they intone the goodbye. I gotta go. The voices echo each other, the voices love each other.

And the rap that Karl does about being in jail and 'hustling from behind'. What the hell is that about?

And why the hell will no one take Wilson's claims seriously?

Someone at *NME* likes it. My God. They want to interview Shaun and Karl together.

Great. The Factory promotion team go into action. Only problem: Karl's doing cabaret in Jersey. OK, we fly Shaun, Nathan and the *NME* to Jersey. When you're hustling genius, no expense spared. It's all set for a Monday morning. The group also have a TV appearance in London on the Tuesday, but that's cool. Shaun will fly back to London on Monday afternoon.

10.35am, Monday, it's Nathan on the phone from a call box at Jersey airport.

'Don't know what happened, we're coming through customs and they search Shaun's bag and he says he doesn't know what it's doing there but there's a little plastic bag and traces of white powder and he says he has no idea where it came from but they've carted him off and...'

'Fucking hell,' says Wilson, shocked, worried and half relieved that nothing changes, that excitement and controversy live and flourish in his crazy world.

Nabs and Wilson discuss the practicalities. Getting a lawyer, getting in court, getting the rest of the band down to London overnight. They go to work.

3.15pm, Monday, it's Nathan on the phone from his Jersey hotel room.

'We're in court tomorrow morning at 10.00am, I've got a lawyer over here and he says we could get bail, but we can't get to see Shaun. Apparently he's refusing to see anybody.'

'Je-e-e-sus, just keep trying. The band are on the way down to London. Horse-man seems to have it under control. Ring me when you see Shaun.'

10.15pm, Monday, it's Nathan on the phone again. Nothing to say. Shaun still refusing to see them.

9.35am, Tuesday, it's Nathan again; they're heading for court and still haven't seen the boy. Fingers crossed. Send the band to the TV studio. There's a flight out to Heathrow at 11.00am. Fingers crossed.

10.20am, Tuesday, it's Nathan on the phone from Jersey airport.

'We've got bail, he's out, we're going to make the flight, we're OK.'

'Why the fuck wouldn't he see anybody? What was his problem?'

'I'll ask. Gotta rush and get the plane.'

NME never got the interview with Karl and Shaun. But they got a story.

Flying over the English Channel, Shaun was looking out the window, when Nathan thought it was time to clear up some matters.

'Shaun, why wouldn't you see us last night? Why wouldn't you see the lawyer?'

'Whaddya mean? I never refused to see no one. I always see my brief.'

And turned to look back out of the window. Nathan settled into the thinly upholstered seat of the ten-seat plane. Being a little confused and lost was just part of managing the Mondays, going with the flow, the essence of the job.

After a few more minutes' flying time, Shaun turned to his manager.

'I tell you what, them pigs in Jersey are fucking weird. Fucking weird.'

'What do you mean?' asked Nabs.

'Well, they kept offering me a drink.'

'What do you mean, a drink?'

'They kept opening the cell door and asking if I wanted an Advocaat. I told them to fuck off.'

Nathan nodded, turned to face the front of the plane. Just smiling, not saying a fucking thing.

Is this our W.B. Yeats, is this our T.S. Eliot? You bet your fucking life it is.

52

TOKYO, PARIS, NEW YORK, KISS MY ARSE

The cause was a good one. The Mondays, a band to fight for. And as things started to look up for Wilson, he had found a solution to the travails of the day job. The way that Manchester had started to look at itself in the eighties, courtesy of its vital role in the world of rock and roll, was beginning to infiltrate other areas of local culture.

No longer some apologetic has-been of history, a conurbation a century or more out of date, the Factory town was on the up. For three years, every band that wanted to be a band sounded like Joy Division; for the next five years, every band that wanted to be a band sounded like the Smiths. The rest of the country was still coming to terms with the architectural glory of the nightclub on Manchester's Whitworth Street. When they figured it out, they would build the second, third and fourth Superclubs.

If you're in the lead in youth culture, you are in the lead in the thing that leads. Which means that Leeds is nowhere and neither is Tokyo or Los Angeles.

There was a self-confidence, a sense of global style that made the kids feel alright. On top of the world. Exactly.

Even before the soon-to-come dawn of Acid House, Wilson had his proof of the change when escorting a 'famous' artist around town one night after a profile on *Granada Reports*, the local TV news show which still gave Wilson face time. The artist was Oldham-born, and long-gone

Oldham-left. Bases in London and Los Angeles, the last job a major stained-glass window for Riyadh Airport. He was in Manc for a home-town retrospective in Oldham's civic gallery.

He bought Wilson supper and Wilson in return took him down the Hac. It was a Friday night. Not packed. Upstairs half empty, but the Gay Traitor cocktail bar was heaving. This may have been something to do with the free drinks distributed by the bar staff, but Wilson couldn't tell 'cause he paid for his drinks. Setting a good example was the name of the game. But for no one else. Wilson finally found out about the free-drinks-for-all-in-the-Gay-Traitor-except-him scam when he was being interviewed for a 'life as a drunk' documentary in 1998. Never mind.

Back in 1985, said Oldham artist developed a puzzled look. Sipped his Jack and Coke in a bemused manner. Finally he turned to Wilson.

'I'm sorry, I've been away for ten years, I know, but I don't understand this. I left a run-down mill town and never looked back. I live a bit of a jet-set lifestyle. I go to parties in Paris and Los Angeles and... everywhere. But these kids, these kids from my home town, are brighter, better-dressed, cooler, just everything, than anyone I've come across anywhere in the world in the last five years. I'm in shock. What's happened?'

Wilson couldn't answer. Came out with that over-used vagary, 'This is Manchester.'

In all honesty, he knew it was true and would also love to know why.

But that was the way it was and the disease was spreading. Even his bosses at Granada were moving on from the 'Let's do a loony' bits to stuff with more meat.

And that's why the day job was looking up.

Wilson found himself doing small (that's cheap) documentaries, explor-ing the North-West as they called this kingdom whose nerve endings spread out from that millstone-grit spine of the Pennines all the way to the beach, which sounds good, and the cold grey of the Irish Sea, which doesn't, exploring past and present and finding a reason for the future.

It was 16mm Ford Madox Brown.

Visitors to this northern city should be one-wayed into the Great

Victorian Town Hall, noting the much later Town Hall extension and getting in an instant why legendary history professor A.J.P. Taylor said it was the best building in Britain in the first half of the twentieth century – the lines and pitch of the walls, the finish – and moving swiftly on into the old bit, up the sweeping staircases onto the first floor and on into the Great Hall. Not so great a hall, perhaps, but the pictures are top dollar. Some bright spark invited Ford Madox Brown, the pre-Raphaelite number four, to paint great moments from civic history. He chose twelve of them.

Wilson's favourite was the gentleman scientist and draper, Crabtree, with the telescope and expectant look on his face from 1600-and-something. One reason was that the bloke was from Salford, which was cool, and the other was the story of how this rank amateur, in his country house on the Kersal cliffs overlooking the Irwell, read all he could of Copernicus and Kepler, took it all in and figured that on a certain day and at a certain time, the planet Venus would pass across the face of the sun. And it bloody well did.

Wilson made a small, cheap documentary about the Transit of Venus. He also shared the Ford Madox Brown syllabus on John Dalton sitting waiting for some methane to bubble out of the swamp.

And there were the early ones. The Flemish weavers coming to the city in 1363. This WAS the immigrant city. Wilson had long wondered why his grandfather, pure German from the excellent Black Forest city of Freiburg, having emigrated to America in 1900, had come nearer home two years later and settled in Salford. Salford? Where's the bloody sign saying 'Give me your tired, your poor, your huddled masses'? Why, in God's name, Salford?

And then, in doing another documentary, small and cheap, about a Manchester scientist called Chaim Weizmann, he got the gig. Weizmann was a German chemist who came to Manchester, like thousands of other Germans, in the nineteenth century, partly to do their stuff in the textile dyeing business, settled, loved it and told his friends. And they told their friends. Manchester and its environs was the place for Germans to go. You only hear German spoken in the cocktail bar at Manchester's Halle

Orchestra performances today. Whalley Range, a whole district of grand houses on the inner city boundary, was not built, as everyone thought, to provide tree-lined avenues for kerb-crawlers; the red light hung in what a century ago was called Little Germany.

Just like Chinatown in the 1980s, growing, expanding, glowing. If you're leaving southern China and don't fancy the rain coming off the Seattle Sound, the rain in Manchester will do just nicely.

You can even join the Cheshire Hunt like Engels, the old two-timer.

But ask again, and again, why Manchester?

A half-hour profile – sorry – small, cheap documentary, of the textile billionaire David Alliance, big boss of Coates Viyella, answered the question, 'why Manchester?' once and for all. Alliance was answering the question from Wilson the interviewer: 'Why do you, one of Britain's richest industrialists, keep your head office in Manchester and continue to live in Manchester?'

'I'll tell you why.'

Forty years in England had only mellowed the delightful Middle-Eastern lilt of his speech. Alliance was a handsome, charismatic man in his mid-fifties who once tried to warn his friend the Shah of Iran, 'You're feeding their bellies, you've got to start feeding their minds.'

'I'll tell you why. When I had been in this country from my home in Persia no more than ten days, I was looking for my uncle's house in Clyde Road in West Didsbury. I was sheltering from the rain under the awnings of the old Rediffusion cinema in East Didsbury. I spoke maybe ten words of English. I had the address on a piece of paper. I saw a woman pushing a pram, I showed her the address and she indicated I should follow her. We walked, perhaps a mile and a half, through the rain, and finally got to Clyde Road and got to my uncle's house. I knocked. He opened the door and flung his arms round me, shouting, "Davoud, Davoud." And I looked back and the woman waved and walked back the way we had come, pushing the pram.

'I turned to my uncle and said, "She wasn't coming this way, why did she come all this way if she wasn't coming this way?"

"Davoud, because this is Manchester."'

It is this city's hospitality to the outside that gives rise to the great truism of Manchester music: Manchester kids have the best record collections. That's not a Wilson line, though he wishes it was. He'd been given this gem by A&R hero Dave Ambrose. Right on, Dave. They do. They have the best record collections. Open to outside influences.

Why do you think Jon Dasilva, Graeme Park and the Pick were playing house music on a Friday night? Why were the Mondays listening to it every fucking night? It was bloody foreign, wasn't it. It was and this is the city of the foreigner, with its open arms. And hands held out, palm up?

And maybe that's why so many of the people in this book are mysteriously devoted to the town. Its open arms inspire a return. Even down to putting everything you've earned and everything you're going to earn into a designer dance hall that was now slowly approaching break-even thanks to student (urgh) night and Stella a quid a pint.

And you never give up. That was the lesson of Wilson's next small, cheap documentary. The story of the Manchester Ship Canal.

King Cotton made us first city of the empire. Foundation stone of the Industrial Revolution. Bit like Peter Saville being responsible for Designer Britain. Good thing or bad? Maybe like Chou En-Lai said when asked the same question about the French Revolution: it's too soon to tell.

Anyway, come the American Civil War and all this cotton stuff comes to a halt. Famously, the textile workers of England's North-West sided with the black (Liverpool-imported, if you don't mind) slaves and Lincoln's Republican army, although this was precisely against their own interests, holding down jobs that relied on the plantation owners of the South. They rightly identified the African slave labour as remarkably similar to their own alienated labour.

A little bit Bradley Hardacre and a little bit Andy Warhol.

When the war was over and it was time to get back to work, sea transport had become the central economic factor in delivery and commerce. You had to be a port. And our friends down the road did bloody well. To this day Liverpool has civic buildings and a built environment of real pride constructed when it ruled the waves.

Manchester was on the skids. But did they give up? Does the Pope shit in the woods? They decided they'd have a Port of Manchester. 'You're thirty-five miles from the sea, you fools', yelled *Punch* magazine, 'we'll have the port of Birmingham next.'

Fuck off.

We built the Manchester Ship Canal. Opened, with a party, in 1894. Bloody great liners could enter the canal just near Ellesmere Port on the south side of the Mersey Bay and sail via locks to the Port of Manchester.

But they didn't. None of 'em. No passing trade. Bit like the early years of the Haçienda. You see, what was there to go there for (not the Hac, the Port of Manchester)? (Did I tell you the Port of Manchester was in Salford? Thought you should know.) All the modern factories to process modern goods had been built in Liverpool 'cause that's where the action was. So not much point in navigating those locks, then. Not really.

As you've gathered, the Hac was still open and the Victorian bunch weren't shitting out either. 'Let's build a place near the canal that is just for industry. We'll give it wide roads and build railway lines into each factory site.'

Trafford Park is the world's first industrial estate and yes, you've guessed it. They built it and they came – ships, oceans of them. The port prospered, and the young Wilson would walk beside the dock wall in the late fifties, hand firmly held by the old lady from round the corner who had two season tickets for the Main Stand at United, looking up from the pavement stalls selling rattles and scarves and red plastic player badges, at the prows of the ocean-going liners that stretched over the dock wall and hovered directly overhead like the beaks of great metal bird-like things. This simile is running out of steam but those prows were bird-like, believe me.

And nearing the ground, Wilson would break away from the old lady's hand now and jump over and trip over the railway sleepers that the adults were too sensible to jump; jumping and tripping over the secret marketing ingredient of Trafford Park: everyone's right to their own railway line.

All this stuff, all these small, cheap documentaries, are all part of the context, and sure made the day job more acceptable. Wilson was in his element. His TV stuff and his music stuff merged in one big Patriot Game. If you can make the best pop songs, then you can do anything, and the city that can invent the computer and the industrial revolution can invent the next youth revolution.

53

BLISS IT WAS IN THAT DAWN TO BE ALIVE BUT TO BE YOUNG WAS VERY HEAVEN

Let's scrub that bit at the end of the last chapter. No one except the youth invent the next youth revolution. 'Trust the kids,' says Ian Brown, 'I went to school with some of them.'

But someone has to do the groundwork and that someone was a youth called Paul Cons. Remember that committee that ran the Hac, the dumb-as-shit committee of clever people? Well, their last desperate act on the eve of the arrival of the long-haired one from Nottingham was to appoint this boy as 'promotions assistant', whatever the hell that meant. Consie, as we shall know him, while not resolutely gay, was arty and as switched on as a 150-watt light bulb. His first action was to instigate Zumbar night. It was arty. As was the name, and don't ask where the fuck it came from, 'cause I have no bloody idea.

At least it was a stylish counterthrust to bloody student night.

And then, at one of those interminable management meetings where Gretton and Wilson discussed matters that are best defined as ancient history, with the usual zealous passion, the kid Cons said he wanted to do an Ibiza night, please. This was early spring 1988. Obviously, Cons had been out the previous summer as Ecstasy overload spread from the '86 contingent of workers, DJs and proppers to the general tanked-up community of '87, and felt that giving a bit of summer stuff to the punters before and after their cheap flights to Ibiza Town airport could do a bit of business.

OK, said the big bosses, with nary a thought as they got back to discussing who put the stage in the wrong bloody place and why Wilson's choice of 'Round And Round' as the second single off the recent New Order album had been a fucking disaster and Wilson promising that he would never put his hand up in a board meeting ever again.

Cons got on with it, which meant hiring a portable swimming pool and getting a large, round wooden sign made, inscribed with a burning sun and the letters H, O and T.

The swimming pool was a big, round canvas-sided tub that could and did fit a dozen dance fiends at one go. Bloody stupid, eh? Didn't they know that lots of water after Ecstasy could drown you? No they didn't. Those tragic stories were still in the undreamed-of future.

'Hot' got going in mid-May.

Wilson had been away on an early summer break and on homecoming had a call to suggest he check out the Wednesday nights pretty damn quick. Did so. Walked in that next week and before he got to the main bar, which required a long walk along the full length of the dance floor, the adrenalin was pumping and pumping and pumping.

On the dance floor, maybe a hundred punters, no more. Half a dozen of said punters were atop podiums, basic black, round go-go dancer bits about five feet high. All were doing something, a kind of dancing. But the movements were all from the shoulders and arms. It's what happens when you're a little too far out – moving your feet would be dangerous and even ungainly. Arms were raised in the air, rolling and touching and pushing in sync to the pulsing beats, a radical blend of the Friday-night fare from Chicago and Detroit.

But to hell with the dance, look at the eyes.

Bushy tailed and bright as fuck. A simple excitement burned in two hundred pupils. A simple excitement that Wilson had seen before. It was more than just the E, it was something else.

Although the faces were more attractive than that cataclysmic night in the Lesser Free Trade Hall – the drooping jaws of the 1976 audience were deeply unattractive – the things three inches higher up were identical. The eyes. The same simple excitement and sense of brilliant self-containment.

'What have we here,' he said, in the manner of someone finding what only now he realizes he has been searching for all his life. Wilson gazed at the gazes in happy shock.

At the end of the night, this precious few, this band of brothers (and sisters – Barney's girlfriend Sarah was giving it everything that night, with a silver New York whistle lodged between her lips) turned to the DJ box, raised arms even higher, saluted, cheered, clapped and, in Sarah's case, whistled.

There's something happening here.

The rest is not silence but history, something Channel 4 can make six-part documentaries about.

The Mondays' associates were now doing the Amsterdam run on a serious level. And the drug had found its music.

The world was not conquered that season. 'Hot' night grew, slowly, but with increasing excitement and general joy. It's like when people grow dope plants at home. Before you put the little leafy tree under the fluorescent sun in that upstairs cupboard, there's the germination bit, the wet tissue, the seed, the sprouting and the first chlorophyll steps. None of the majesty of the fork-leafed foliage, but the faint wet-green wonder of early nature. The summer of '88 was germination time.

And the spring and summer of '89 were for the flowering.

Everything came together.

Bit like being part of the French Revolution, I gather, from what people said who were at the French Revolution.

piecetocam

See, they applauded the DJ. Not the musician, not the creator, not the music, but the medium. This is it. This is the day the music died. This is the birth of Rave culture, of the beatification of the beat, welcome to the Dance Age. This is the moment when even the white man starts dancing. This is Manchester.

54
YVETTE DAWN LIVESEY

Wilson's cyclical theory of human culture had been fairly on the button so far. Luck, or educated guess? Your call, reader. But for a man whose ego-drive was about being right, the ego was growing. What else could go right? Well, the Mondays could break, but patience, patience. Well, what about sex and romance? What could happen in this truly central part of the life of this educatedly lucky guy?

Loads.

'Tony, it's Charles, everything OK?'

Ah yes, the day job. Never give up the day job, and here's why.

These years of wonderment in the life of Factory and the Haçienda were achieved while – and perhaps because – Wilson was spending eight hours a day in Liverpool fronting the new Granada regional news from the coolly regenerated Albert Dock. His double life gave rise to questions from the big bosses back in Quay Street Manchester, questions like, 'What is this bloody place of his, the Hallucienda or whatever they call it?' – I feel a famous Saville poster coming on – and 'What's Wilson doing at the moment, apart from using our bloody phones to run his bloody business?'

Right now he was using their phones to talk to his producer Charles, who was asking a favour.

'There's this girl who's interested in a TV presenting career, she's a friend of a friend of mine who works for BBC local radio. Said I'd give her a tour round the news centre but I've got to get back for a budget meeting in Manchester, so I wondered if you'd show her round. She's due in about 10.30am. Oh, and she's Miss England, I think, and Miss UK as well.'

'No?'

Wilson was always saying no to Charles. In this tiny professional outpost of his life, as the TV presenter, Wilson chose to remain the talent, 'the meat' as Americans call it. Being difficult. It's what's expected of talent. In the rest of his life he was the working boss coping with difficult artists. The complete role reversal here in Granadaland helped an easy mental separation between the night job and the day job. And in the day job, he always said no to Charles.

Except this time.

Whaddayouthink?

This is a book and it's a bit late in the day to complain about the inadequacies of the word 'beautiful'. But to say that this twenty-year-old who arrived at the Albert Dock that morning was beautiful... Pointless and insufficiently descriptive.

But it wasn't that that got this stunning girl under his skin. As he guided young beauty around the news centre, there were the usual trappings of minor celebrity.

'Hello, Tony,' said the lovely Liverpool dinner ladies.

'Alright, T,' said the doormen.

He turned to the lady of dreams.

'You can never judge a book by its cover, I always say. And you've got a very nice cover, if you'll forgive me being so open. First edition. Very collectable.'

'Nice to see you, Tony...' wafted again from a bunch of locals across the corridor.

'Hi.'

'And what do you do?' said Yvette, the aforementioned twenty-year-old, with polite curiosity.

Wilson thinks for a moment.

'Er, I'm... Tony Wilson.'

'How do you mean?' she followed, equally at a loss for the direction of this conversation. 'Your job here?'

'Well, I'm Tony Wilson.'

Another pause.

Oh my God, she must only watch BBC. Oh, God. What a prat.

'It's a bit chilly,' she said, catching the mood of the moment with precision.

'Have this.' And with a quick unfurling of one of his trademark scarves from around his neck, he got the event back on line.

'Thank you,' she said, interestingly slowly, and with the prettiest smile he had ever seen.

'Keep it, it's cashmere, course, least I can do for Miss UK. I haven't got a tiara, so you'll have to make do with that, sweetheart.'

He continued in a new and expansive vein. 'Granada's just my hobby. My proper job... have you heard the Happy Mondays? I look after them. Factory Records, my label, and New Order, heard of them?'

'Yes, of course.'

There you go. 'Sometimes even the Haçienda, do you know the Haçienda?'

'Of course, fantastic.'

'Well I own it, well part own it. If you ever want reduced admission come and see me – better still, you get in free if you escort me. I'm flirting, by the way.'

'Yes, you are,' she said, with another of those smiles.

'It's that obvious?' he echoed.

'It is.'

piece**to**cam

Now reader, please don't judge. Piety is a very unattractive virtue. Flirting is a very natural process. She was aware of it. He was aware of it. He was being post-modern before it was fashionable.

And by the way, I know what you're thinking. Forty-year-old hipster in baggy Comme Des Garcons sucking up to the best thing ever to walk down a Chanel catwalk. Well they're still together, just, twelve years on. So whatever you were thinking, you're wrong.

When they made the movie of Wilson's story they planned to put a sex scene in, but probably couldn't manage the truth and gave up. How could any movie describe the passion that had so surprised Livesey and Wilson and glued the unlikely couple together, sticky, gushingly wet, and utterly obsessed. The movie people didn't try but left in a post-coital conversation between the lovers which may or may not have taken place, but which advances our story just a little.

'You know, I think that Shaun Ryder is on par with W.B. Yeats as a poet,' says Wilson, lying back in bed.

'Really?'

'Absolutely. Totally.'

'Well that's amazing, as everybody else thinks he's a fucking idiot.'

And we'll save the sex stuff for another book.

55

AN EXPENSIVE BARRISTER IS NEARLY AS GOOD AS SEX ANYWAY

Life in Manchester was becoming the ultimate fairground. And the Haçienda was the cathedral of this new life. The arching ceiling that had given the guys the worst acoustic problems since Beethoven's hearing was now so gothically correct. The hands, voices and spirits raised in the air, rising high into the roof girders and thence on to heaven.

But the whirling adventure began to resemble the merry-go-round in that Hitchcock movie. Round and round, faster and faster, faster and faster till, careering, it looks as if it may break off its pivot, may and will spill over into destruction of riders and ridden.

To mix metaphors, and auteurs, and since everything comes back to Yeats, things began to fall apart. The centre, indeed, could not hold. For somewhere at the centre was THE drug and Greater Manchester Police were becoming unamused.

They were watching, they were waiting.

And finally it came.

The awful, awful case of Claire Leighton. It didn't matter that she bought her supplies in Stockport, didn't matter that, like everybody else, she consumed the pill outside the confines of the Haçienda, maybe in the queue like so many others.

What mattered was that she collapsed on the Haçienda dance floor, was taken to hospital and suffered a grotesque death. First Ecstasy death in Britain. Not the kind of first you want. For the next ten years, the news of any Ecstasy death anywhere in the UK was greeted by the *Manchester Evening News* with a side feature, majoring on two library pics. Claire Leighton and Anthony Wilson.

That was the way it was going, and Greater Manchester Police were going for the jugular.

A closing-down order was delivered, removal of license and forty-seven reasons why.

First thing, pacify the police by increasing security to virtual strip search. In a way, the Thursday management meeting accepted that the only way to stay open was to kill the culture, or at least maim it. Anything, anything.

Second thing, get a good barrister.

Alan, Rob, Tony, Barney and Hooky gathered on a Monday morning in the offices of their (criminal) solicitor on Manchester's Deansgate. They waited. For the star turn to arrive.

George Carman swept through the meeting room doors with arms outstretched and assistant following with boxes of papers.

'Good morning, gentlemen, how wonderful to be back in Manchester. As you know, I pursued much of my early career in this fine town and it's a real pleasure to be back.'

He had the appearance of a victorious Roman general, re-entering the Senate after a particularly successful overseas campaign. His arms were open as much in welcome to himself as to the assembled clientele.

The gang said hello to the most famous barrister this side of the O.J. Simpson case.

'Now, first things first. On the train up, I had a first browse of the papers and I have one very important first piece of advice.'

Dramatic pause. He did them pretty well, did George.

'*He* shuts the fuck up.'

His glance went straight down the table. Wilson blanched. Began to shuffle uncomfortably in his seat as Gretton led the response.

'We told you it was your fault, for fuck's sake. We told you, we told you.'

Absolutely correct surmise, George. The great barrister had rightly identified the fact that Wilson's persistent crowing to the media about the glories of this new youth culture, were seen not as a paean to the cultural glories of a baggy music style that took the rolling rhythms of the new black music from America into the attitude-driven glories of Manchester rock, but as an espousal of the necking of copious quantities of a lethal DRUG.

Greater Manchester Police had a small-time Timothy Leary on their hands, they thought, and they were out to stop it, with the Home Office, presumably and correctly horrified by Claire Leighton's tragic death, also on their case.

Needless to say, Wilson shut the fuck up.

And whether it was the threat of Carman, the temporary stifling and dismantling of the culture on the Haçienda door, or maybe the eloquent letter of support from Leader of Manchester City Council, Graham Stringer, who valued what the loonies from 86 Palatine Road were up to as part of his grand regeneration plan for the city; whichever and whatever, after six months Greater Manchester Police backed off and rescinded the closure order.

Survival, exhalation of breath.

Exhalation of large quantities of money. How much do you think George Carman costs?

And the real problem with the Haçienda was that it was still not making money. Even before they tightened the door. Fuck it, it never made any money. There were huge crowds and a great atmosphere, but it was all fuelled by Ecstasy, not alcohol, and they didn't sell E at the bar.

Though they did talk about it.

They were spending money on the staff, the building, the DJs and the sound system, but most of the money spent by the revellers went to the drug dealers. And guess what? They didn't pass the E money on to Wilson and Gretton. These inconsiderate people spent the money on clothes and cars and girls and houses.

Which I suppose is urban regeneration.

COMMUNIQUÉ

WINTER 90/91

Dear Friend

Let's face it, 1990 has not been
an easy year for The Haçienda.

Our problems began in May with the threat to our
license when we had no choice but to take drastic
action in order to keep the club open.

A major problem which we have also had to deal
with is the increase in violence in and around
Manchester's clubs. This is an extremely worrying
development to which there is no easy solution.

It must be apparent to you that both these factors
have seriously affected the way The Haçienda is run.

We realise that things like searches on the door,
video surveillance and high profile security,
while necessary, have had a damaging effect
on the club's atmosphere and we would be the
first to admit that we have found it difficult to
get the balance right between law
enforcement and partying.

We are particularly aware that the door policy
at The Haçienda has provoked much criticism.
One problem has been that on occasion regular
customers have been turned away. We aim to
remedy this situation in the New Year with a
membership scheme for Saturday nights which will
ensure that regulars are guaranteed admission at a
discount price (details will be announced shortly).

However we feel that it is worth remembering
that the much maligned Haçienda door staff *are*
under a lot of pressure and while they may not
always get it right they are having to work in a
difficult situation and *do* deserve your support.

So, our court hearing approaches and from
January the 3rd we will get an indication
whether The Haçienda has a future.
We are confident that it does.

To the pessimists, piss off.

TO ALL OF YOU WHO HAVE CONTINUED TO
SUPPORT US THROUGH THESE DIFFICULT TIMES,
WE WOULD LIKE TO SAY A BIG THANK YOU

56
CALL THE COPS

Something had to change. And it did.

Remember the drug dealers and their protectors who at the end of the last chapter were spending their money on clothes and cars and girls and houses? Well, now they started spending the money on clothes and cars and girls and houses and guns. And then more guns. And more guns.

Mason and Wilson asked for an urgent meeting with the cops.

For two hours they tried to explain what they saw as their problem.

'You see, there's one gang who just re-equipped. The Cheetham Hill lot. They've got new Uzi's and everything. Well they did a walk round town a few weeks ago. Remember when you closed The Gallery, well they all moved over to us and the other clubs the next weekend, in particular us. They just opened their overcoats at the door, showed the pretty new metal and explained that they were coming in as they were now Haçienda VIPs, Manchester VIPs.'

The police were extremely interested in drugs and guns, and the conversation might have gone something like this:

'Who is Mike Pickering?'

'Pardon?'

'Who is Mike Pickering?'

'What the hell has that got to do with armed men demanding free champagne?'

'I repeat, who is Mike Pickering?'

'Je-e-e-sus, he's a DJ, a DJ.'

'Do you have his address?'

And so on, for an hour or more. Mason and Wilson trying to explain that these guys were cocks of the town, cool as Häagen-Dazs, and that if something wasn't done, the rest of the gangs would finally cotton on and get tooled up.

'Who is Mike Pickering?'

'Sir, if you don't get on the case, handguns are going to replace trainers as this town's primary fashion item.'

'Who is…'

It appears that ACPO, the then newly created national social club for UK police chiefs, seen by some as a kind of effete British P2 for those with memories of Italian Masonry (and we're not talking the walls of St Peter's), had just set up their Rave Unit to combat illicit drug dancing. The only thing they knew for certain about this subterranean culture was that the words 'Mike' and 'Pickering' appeared on 73% of all rave flyers.

And our man was under orders.

'Who is…'

Ignoring this for the umpteenth time, the Hac management moved into practical mode.

'Listen, we need help, sir. We work a lot in America, in tough clubs in big American cities. We often find that they employ one or two proper policeman on their doors. Full cops. And it works. Could we…'

'We can't do that. We don't do that.'

'But you do it at football matches. We'd pay.'

'That's different.'

'How different?'

'Er, it's just different.'

And so Wilson and Mason walked away empty handed. They knew they had to be connected, connected to someone who would protect them and their staff and their customers in the storms to come.

And so, if they couldn't connect with the forced of law and order, it was on to the forces of law and disorder.

Their nerves were jangling. Their trusty head doorman, Roger – a peaceful, powerful man and connected to Cheetham Hill as someone who could read their letters and get them lawyers – had had enough. Told

Mason that five years of sleeping with a gun under his pillow was more than enough and that retirement beckoned.

'After Christmas.'

Fuck, what kind of New Year was this to be?

First idea, try out a bunch of highly respected London security. Run by brothers who sported matching scars and the toughest of appearances. Gentle giants with the vital ability to glaze over their pupils with the possibilities of serious violence when needed. Ace guys. Ace team.

But not from Manchester.

Red rag? This was a fucking large red blanket to every team north and south of the city centre.

Two weeks in, a Cheetham Hill sub-head went walkabout in the Hac entrance. Waving a gun in the air. Shots were fired.

Fucking hell. So much for outside security.

A hasty board meeting.

Wilson was in Trade Union mood. Several years of being an NUJ Father of Chapel suggested Industrial Action.

'We shut the club for three months. Go on strike. Show them what they'll be missing if they keep fucking with us.'

Gretton didn't like it, but things were so bad he sat there quietly.

Erasmus led the debate on direct-action possibilities. By the time the ins and outs of drug runs from North Africa for financing, sourcing hit men in Las Vegas, and the absolute necessity of moving all family members to another country for nine months had been exhausted, the assembled crowd, who had thought that they were in the music business, were also exhausted. Wilson got his way.

The three months' strike, removing their labour and THE club from the city that deserved it did its business, calmed things down. Slightly.

And there was a hell of a re-opening night.

Gretton and Wilson arrived together. They were excited by the number of cars parked down Whitworth Street. Always a good sign. They were excited by the number of punters in the queue, the blessed queue. Almost more than inside the club, the happy-as-fuck queue that would line up and snake round over the canal bridge, was the social centre, the meeting point, the Agora. Something to do with worrying about getting those little pills lost in an overzealous search by the doorman. So they'd swallow early, and how often, with the queue so slow, would they go up while still outside. Which is probably why nobody complained about the queue. Which is why people loved it. Which is why Consie used to put special entertainment on. Which is why a fanzine, *Freaky Dancing*, was written for the queue.

The queue.

But tonight, the queue was complaining. This time they hadn't been waiting so long they went up before they got in; this time it was so long some of them had started coming down.

The partners walked quickly to the door, greeted by a scene of confusion and argument and assailed by a high-pitched whooping sound that came from no freaky dancer.

They'd done a bit of redesign for the grand reopening. Ben Kelly had redone the H-bone iron stakes, the dance-floor pillars, with new colours for the brandiloquent angled lines of colour that occupied the upper reaches. Still a bit of yellow and black. Just less yellow and black. And more red.

And the other addition was the metal detector, a great big steel and wood electronic arch placed just past the box-office window. This would keep out the guns and knives. This would guarantee the future.

Well, it was re-opening night and the future was going whoooop whoooop fucking continuously. Gretton and Wilson muscled in and asked their doormen what the fuck was going on.

'It's a metal detector.'

'We know it's a metal detector. That's why we bought it and had it put up. To detect metal.'

'Yes, but the floor's metal, all metal. Whoever walks through, it detects the metal and fucking goes off. You've built it over a steel floor, boss.'

Gretton sighed. Long and deep.

Wilson looked lost a moment, then laughed.

'Well that was a great way to spend £7,000, Rob.'

Rob's second sigh was longer and deeper.

That night, Gretton got behind a bunch of lagers. If he couldn't drown Wilson he could drown how he made him feel.

He stared at his partner, and pointed a shaky finger towards Wilson's chest.

'You know your trouble, Tony? You don't know what you are. I fucking know what you are, but you don't know what you are.'

'My curiosity gets the better of me, Rob. Tell me, what am I?'

Gretton rolled his answer around for a long time before he leaned forward and, in the gravest tones, continued:

'You're a cunt.'

'Well I knew that, Rob, that was something I did know.'

This scene is here to remind you that this is a book about mates. As Gretton once explained the entire project to a young acolyte who wanted to know what was the secret of Factory and the Haçienda: 'I just put out some records with me mates.'

And his mate was a cunt. But then his mate knew it.

57
THINK ABOUT THE FUTURE

It wasn't all bad news. The dogged perseverance with the Mondays paid off. And Nabs did a good job. As the guys expected. Just kept coming up with ideas.

'Hey, I've got a contact with Vince Clark. Why don't we get Vince to do a remix of "Wrote For Luck" and re-release it?'

The original rolling rock Hannett spectacular that was 'WFL' had come out in December and sold 1,500 copies. Bit crap, really. Lost money. Didn't sell the album.

But this was a good idea and so it happened.

Truly great pop-house mix that begins to bring out the rhythms buried back in Driffield in that blacked-out vinyl-carpeted den.

Great single, sold 1,500. Well crap, really. Lost money. Didn't sell the album.

'Hey, I've been talking to these DJ mixers, Oakenfold and Osborne. Why don't we get them to do another mix of "Wrote For Luck". And re-release it?'

This is almost a year on from release one. But it was a good idea and so it happened.

Great single, only sold 1,500 on release. But it was a great single. And it sold 1,500 the next week too. And it sold 1,500 the next week too. And it sold 2,000 the first week of October. And 2,500 the second week of October and...

Remember the refrain: in a world of billboards and bollocks, a shining star peeks out of the top of the dung-heap. The song. The fucking song. A great song will rise up just because it's a great fucking song. In a world of hype there is, in the end, only honesty.

And the 'Think About the Future' mix of 'Wrote For Luck' was a fucking classic. Hypnotic, rolling, it was the aural equivalent of that unique spectacle of the House Revolution. A room, a club, a stadium where every bastard was moving, every body in motion, from bar staff to podium dancer, everyone. At the Hac, the pot-collectors moved to the beat as they brushed their way into Acid Corner, pushing through the first three ranks standing, moving, dancing on the two steps up into the biggest of the Haçienda's big alcoves, where they were protected from prying Special Branch eyes. And they'd dance and move as they picked their way through the boys and girls, sitting on what was left of Alvar Aalto, rolling joints incessantly, and the arms and hands that held Rizla were moving dancing and all the seated bodies swayed and danced as they sat.

That was the sound of the 'Think About the Future' mix of 'Wrote for Luck'. It was the sound of the dance, a gentle pounding that got to the cervical cortex. Otherwise known as an anthem.

And anthems sell over a long period, particularly to every bugger back from his hols. And anthems can break groups and this one broke the Mondays.

Hallelujah.

That was the follow-up single.

piece**to**cam

But this is not my story, I'm not Prince Hamlet, nor was ever meant to be. This is not a book about me. I'm a minor character in my own story. Truly Dickensian hero, bit of a wally, bit of a cipher, surrounded by bizarre and larger-than-life characters. This is about the music and the people who made the music, Ian Curtis and Shaun Ryder and Martin Hannett.

Death puts it into perspective; we're all equal in the grave. Except Martin. He was a large person and huge talent. And like other characters in this tale, he went and died. And his coffin wouldn't fit in the grave. Martin Hannett, too big for death. And too big for his heart. Couldn't cope with the extra ten stone. Couldn't cope with other things, maybe. Dead and buried in a wind-swept south Manchester cemetery. When they finally got the coffin in the ground. It wasn't till a year or so later that I cried. But I cried a lot that day. Cried a lot.

58
HOW DO YOU
DO THOSE
THINGS TO ME?

And so the wheel turned again. The Haçienda chilled out for a while and Wilson was back in a Mustang. The 1990 Ford Mustang is a joke, a wonderful joke. A Ford Escort with a soft top and a five-litre engine. As silly and as lovely as Los Angeles itself.

The Budget Rent-a-Car specialty lot in Marina Del Rey did the best deals on Mustangs. Just ten minutes' cab ride north of LAX. Get the plastic swiped, pile the bags in the boot and then up onto La Cienaga, the road from plane to shining plain, the avenue that is the Englishman's mystical entrance to the dreamland, rightly winding you through those nodding donkeys, the primitive oil-drilling rigs that hang out on the scrub hillside, and nod and say hello and lots of stuff besides – echt LA – and the road that soon after gives you your first view of the Hollywood Hills, a few miles further on.

He'd done it before, a number of times. But this time he had the most beautiful woman in the world in the seat next to him. And his band, the Mondays, were working. Hard at it in the Ciudad of our Lady of the Angels of Porciuncula. Even as he drove he knew that to the right of those hills, over where the lights of mid-Hollywood meet the black hole of the Cahuenga Pass, there was a landmark, an icon, the white tower that was the Capitol building. An office building made of 360-degree white balconies perched one on top of the other like a series of ivory concrete parasols. A beautiful thing. And he knew that in the basement of the great Capitol building, in the Capitol studios where Sinatra and the rest had done it, the Happy Mondays with their partner-producers, Oaky and Osborne, were recording their third album. He knew they were all indoors working 'cause he'd rung from the airport. He had been obviously surprised.

The last time he had brought them to the States, the cab from JFK was passing Union Square on the way to the hotel. Three of them got out and he lost them for two whole days. And it was a two-day trip. But now they were working. Actually at it. Apparently the session was on a roll.

Settling into the Sunset Marquis suite, which is not as grand as it sounds, but wonderful in an everyday rock-and-roll sort of way, Yvette undressed and put on the pink Marquis towelling bathrobe. The most beautiful woman in the world in the national colour of Los Angeles. Definitive.

We've already apologized for not doing sex scenes in this book.

And anyway, you'll get the idea if you leave Yvette in bed to recover from the flight and head off with Wilson in the Mustang, at midnight, down Fountain, the back route out of West Hollywood moving east and avoiding the midnight ramblers on Sunset.

Turn left onto Vine and it's straight up.

Into the Capitol car park.

'Just said Factory Records and the guy waved me in and there's loads of parking. Fucking great,' muttered Wilson, remembering to kick down on something he understood to be a footbrake.

Down to the bowels of the building. Warm greetings and hugs from all. The Active Service Unit, as Martin used to call it. A big bunch of the family, in a foreign city, doing it. Gigging, recording, doing stuff. Those Active Service bits were worth all the shit.

'Listen to this T,' said Shaun, excitedly.

'Go on, Steve, run it.'

This time, there wasn't the usual 'But it's not finished yet,' 'We haven't done this or that' or whatever and everyone being precious before someone plays the unmixed recording to the man who signs the cheques. None of it. Easy smiles, the tape turns and the beat that Wilson had heard from the corridor reappeared and went right to his balls. Because it was sex, a piece of music that was pure sex.

'What do you want to hear when we're making love?'

'Let me take you from behind,' and many more Ryder intimacies set against this track that was just sex.

Listen.

▶▶|

Pills 'N' Thrills And Bellyaches, for such was the title of this magnificent collection, did good business. Great business.

It must be fun to have success. Even with shit. You know, market the fuck out of some half-decent bollocks and have a hit, have a big financial hit. But to have success with wonderful art. That is something else altogether, a real heart-and-soul job.

Take the lead single from said album. 'Kinky Afro'. Appropriate that when it was announced by Nathan as the first single, Wilson, for one, wondered why and presumed it was because it was the first track on the album, a kind of sense.

It went to number five in the UK chart.

Years later, he would hear it played repeatedly at half-time over the Tannoy at Old Trafford, and purr inside. Purring 'cause he was now using this song as the heart of his Shaun Ryder-as-God lecture, and because 'Kinky Afro' did the W.B. Yeats bit for him to a treat.

The opening lines:

Son, I'm thirty.
I only went with your mother 'cause she's dirty

... not only shocked and seared, but allowed Wilson to give out that this was the greatest musing on parenthood since Yeats's 'Prayer for my Daughter'.

232

Which, actually, it fucking is.

And it's more interesting than Yeats in its structure. While the first stanza deals with the announcement by his girlfriend that she's pregnant, and the self-scorn felt by a pure scumbag who surely cannot be a parent, the second verse swings right round into a litany of contempt for his own father. It is remarkable. And it went top ten in the pop charts. That's the fucking beauty of it.

'Yippee, yippee, yi, yi, yay.'

You even get Bruce Willis a couple of years early.

'I'm going to crucify some brother today.'

Shaun was asked by a German interviewer, as the group broke across Europe, just how big can you get.

How big can you get?

'You can get so big they nail you to a piece of wood,' said the Reverend Shaun William Ryder.

59
THE EDIFICE COMPLEX

And now, with things going well, what were they going to do?

Manchester was on the cover of *Newsweek*, and the *Sunday Times* colour supplement, on CNN and Russian TV, and, favourite for Wilson, had a front-page feature in the Calendar section of the *Los Angeles Times*.

Manchester was THE city.

The capital of culture.

So what were they going to do?

They were going to push it. Push it further. Much further. What fucking envelope? We can do anything. Look at the Mondays, look at our dance floor. We can do anything.

I'm not going to go into hubris here. If you know what I'm talking about, fine, if not you should read the next few chapters, no more, and then go back to watching TV.

What were they to do? Well they'd already opened a bar, Manchester's first designer bar, named 'Dry' by Barney. Not because, like the Haçienda, it began to run the company dry... though it did.

And when the Haçienda building came on the market – they'd rented from 1981 – they borrowed a million-plus to buy it.

Exposed? Whaddya mean exposed? Let's really hang our dicks out and build some brand new offices and move out of Palatine Road.

A wonderful, long, two-storey ruin was found by Erasmus, in Charles Street at the back of the BBC and close to the city centre. It was purchased, gutted and rebuilt. By Ben Kelly. The genius of the design and the extent of the overruns were pre-ordained.

'You know the bill of quantities in the estimate?'

'Yeah.'

'Well, we have render down at £20 a ton.'

'Yeah.'

'Well, render is £20 a ton. All render, that is, except blue render, which is £130 a ton.'

'And remind me which render we're using?'

Of course. Blue is a special colour. Blue were the walls of the Haçienda, RAF blue and pigeon blue. We like blue.

One hundred and thirty pounds a ton.

No problem.

No problem going for it.

Big problem paying for it.

Later.

'Cause a recession was on its way. The big downturn. God's timing.

piecetocam

Indeed, timing is everything. When we built the Haçienda, it was too soon, when we built the Factory offices it was too late. It did, however, have a zinc roof, which was very cool, although you could only see it from a helicopter.

The Factory team and New Order strolled through their new headquarters, moving up to the top floor, the crowning gem, reached by an aluminium tunnel hood that rose up at 45 degrees into a spacious, 60-foot long atrium, superb polished wood floor and along the centre, hanging by exposed wires and secured beneath by Kee Klamp bolts and piping, but floating free of the floor... the new boardroom table.

These guys, who loved their meetings, their history lessons, would have a boardroom table commensurate with the high cultural-political content of their discussions.

It looked like a long slit, a long, long, 25-foot long slit with rounded sides tapering at the middle and the ends, and lacquered in two shades of red. A real cunt of a table.

'At last we have a proper office.' And Wilson held out his arms in presentation.

'It's made of MDF, fucking MDF,' said Barney.

'How much was it, this table?' chimed in Hooky.

'It's not material that counts, Barney and Peter. You're paying for design.' Wilson had in fact paid a young Manchester architect and his PR partner for this stunning creation.

'He asked how much,' said Rob, sitting in one of the eight new pastel-coloured Arne Jacobsen chairs.

'Thirty grand,' said Wilson without blinking, as if this was just natural.

'Did you pick the shape?' laughed Barney.

'Thirty grand...' said Hooky.

And Rob said nothing. A long silence. He was counting to ten. Not to instill patience or calm his temper. Rob was counting to ten like Houston does, backwards. He was just making sure every fucking bit of his indignation was running properly and turned on for that moment when, all systems go, he flung the Jacobsen bent wood classic backwards and threw himself sideways, aiming for Wilson's throat.

'You dozy fucking twat.'

Wilson fell backwards away from Gretton's swirling attack, ran backwards, trying, unsuccessfully one must presume, to do this with dignity, while Erasmus leapt between them and tried to hold Rob off and push him back to his seat.

'You stupid bastard, thirty thousand fucking pounds.'

Erasmus had Gretton back in his chair. Wilson edged back around the edge of the duotone red vagina. Approached his chair. But ten feet was too close. Gretton was up again, lunging for his partner, trying like hell to get past Erasmus and strangle the life out of this fucking idiot he was sharing a company with.

'Should we let go of him and not be doing this,' said Erasmus. Very forcefully.

'It's alright, Rob.' Razzer tried the soothing touch.

'Thirty thousand pounds for a fucking table.'

And one last dash forward, Wilson back-pedalling again around the room and Erasmus in desperation screamed with desperate finality:

'Will you stop, for God's sake...'

Order was restored.

As it was in the world economy. Nothing goes up for ever. The eighties boom began to implode. Outside, things were turning bad.

All the money they'd borrowed, encouraged by those lovely members of the British professional classes, the bankers. Made sense. Here, borrow this for your building. Property values can only go up. You borrow, but as the value of your building goes up, your balance sheet shows growth and profit without doing a single fucking thing.

'Yes, please.'

Saville warned Wilson in a phone call from his under-threat London studios. Peter was having it hard, himself, and was seeing the downturn early.

Did Wilson listen? No sign that he did.

But he listened when the accountants explained that their building assets had been worth £1.7 million for the Hac, £1.1m for the Factory Offices and £0.6m for the bar. Mills, folks, millions of pounds, when the accountants explained that they were now worth £1.3 million, £0.8 million and £0.4 million, respectively. And three months later, hey presto, they were worth £0.8 million, £0.5 million and £0.3 million. Are you following this? We're talking millions. Millions of fucking pounds.

And do you know about interest rates? Perfect balance. As the value of the property you've borrowed against goes down, the vig on the stuff you've borrowed goes up. Fucked by equilibrium.

And finally, there's that wonderful phrase, fire sale. Accountants like that phrase. It implies, most successfully, the transience of human life. Sic transit gloria mundi, it's a fire sale. This is what things are really worth. When the shit hits the fan, when everything goes. Now.

Total fire sale value. Millions, around £0.9. Which is great, except you've borrowed £2.5 million and the bastards can ask for it back at any time and any time is when they get nervous. And they were shitting themselves.

As were the customers at the Haçienda.

As Manchester blossomed into a major city, full of its crazed new nightlife, Wilson could be heard making the best of it in the media: 'If we want to be Chicago or New York, we have to accept that it is going to be a bit wild.'

That was for the media. Inside, it was shit. The door was connected – had to be – a matter of survival.

piecetocam

I got the idea from Plutarch's Life of Caesar, where it says, keep your friends close but your enemies closer. The problem is often the solution in a different set of clothes.

Fuck Plutarch.

As Cheetham Hill faded as a force in the town, police clampdown and internal whacking doing their bit to sideline them, Salford rose again.

Like a phoenix.

Salford rose like a great big fucking bird, from the flames of rubbish burning on the Ordsall estate, a great big fucking bird with wild, staring eyes and a beak that would peck your fucking head off if you dared to return its stare.

The designer bars followed the clubs, the cool shops followed the designer bars, and the heads and the young fuckers who sheltered under the head's protection followed all. Getting into the city.

'Nice jacket, mate, nice jacket. Now, I'm going to walk out of here in this jacket, yeah, but if you'd rather I take it off, I will, only, if I do, you'll be seeing some pretty unpleasant people in about half an hour's time, get what I mean, mate?'

And at the centre of it all, the Hac. Ego thing. The best club in the world? We're getting in free. Alright?

Alright.

The costs of protecting the staff and customers had risen as dramatically as the property values had fallen. If there's a real double helix in this fucking story, this is it. Security and property in perfectly counterbalanced spirals. Fucking Factory.

In the year of 1992, the total cost of doormen, the money paid to the bouncers, was £375,000. One year.

And where did security stop and protection start? The guys were lost in that one. They knew that Damien and the guys on the door were putting their lives up each night. How do you value that? Three hundred and seventy-five thousand pounds. OK. And when a bunch of young Salford tried to do the door with knives one night, the Hac head of security – that is, the main connection – went into action and thank God the gun mechanism stuck.

So guys were getting ballied up for you, so how can you begrudge the money? 'Er, here's the envelope, er, we'd kind of like to restock the bar, you know, with drink, but, yes, no, you take the cash, we'll be OK, we can always go teetotal. See you again next week.'

More cash going out, less coming in as the Haçienda customers got tired of the intimidation and then were part of a great mood change as cocaine replaced the bad E that had started doing the rounds.

'I'm not enjoying this. I'm not dancing.'

No, you dozy bugger you're on coke. And so are those lot over in Acid Corner. Sorry, Salford corner.

No complaints.

Except.

'I wouldn't mind paying fucking protection if I got fucking protected,' was the complaint.

'Cause now it was all getting out of hand.

No time for metaphor or simile, gotta make some money, but think of a crocodile and how safe you are on its back. And then the fucker starts shaking.

They were running on empty. Shuffling cash for months between the club and the record company. They had to make some money. They had to release records.

A conversation in Wilson's bespoilered Jag.

'New Order want to record another album,' says Rob, dispassionately.

'Thank God for that,' says his mate.

'In Ibiza.'

'Why, why Ibiza?' As if just interested, but in fact smelling rats and the drainpipes of San Antonio.

'Why not Ibiza?'

Exactly, why not? Company philosophy.

It was done. They went to Ibiza. It took two and a half years.

Two and a half fucking years.

Another conversation in Wilson's bespoilered Jag.

'The Mondays want to make another album.'

'Great, we can do it in Manchester, Hooky's got a new studio, all the gear.'

Nathan seems to be mulling this over. Then, in conspiratorial tones:

'You know Shaun's had a bit of trouble with the brown recently? Well, I've been trying to get him off the smack and onto methadone. But now he's doing both. Both barrels. Well, I've been reading about this place where there isn't any H. It's an island.'

'Wouldn't be the Isle of Man?' Was this said by Wilson in cynicism or hope? Just a little joke, maybe.

'No, Tony, Barbados. No smack on Barbados.'

'Sounds good, Nathan, sounds good.'

And all done for the best possible personal and artistic reasons, and indeed there was no smack on Barbados.

Pity no one pointed out that Barbados was Crack Central.

Rock Island.

Fuck.

60
ANOTHER
GEOGRAPHY LESSON

It's not that it even started well.

The Happy Mondays were never particularly inconspicuous in airport lounges. Lots of barging of trolleys, airport police attention and the like.

But they were on their way to the sun to make their fourth album, and they were all prepared, even down to taking a large bottle of methadone to ease Shaun into clucking in the sun. A large bottle of methadone that was in a brown paper bag that was even now falling sideways off Shaun's trolley.

'Awwww fuck, the meth...' and the bag and the bottle hit the hard marble floor of Terminal Three groundside and shattered. What do passers-by think? How do they experience half a dozen 'musicians', because they all do look like musicians, crawling, howling, on the marble floor, trying to salvage bits of glutinous liquid with curved shards of glass and torn brown paper, all the while, a crazy man screaming something, clearly in personal pain, and waving a hefty sheaf of papers.

'I've got prescriptions, I've got prescriptions.'

▶▶▌

Wilson is back in the Sunset Marquis with Madam. The towelling robes replaced by erotica from the Pleasure Chest on Santa Monica, and the Mustang is the 1991 model.

But the big change is that his boys are in Eddy Grant's studio in Barbados and he's on the phone to Nathan every six hours.

'Sorry, To', they're doing rocks. Lots of rocks. We've lost two hire cars, Bez has broken his arm in five places and Shaun isn't writing any lyrics.'

'Fucking hell. OK, let's cut the PDs.'

This is normal routine practice. Libertinism getting out if hand? Stop the per diems.

This is good, 'cause it reminds you that you did Latin at school and also stops the money supply to the band.

One week later. Another phone call to the Sunset Marquis.

'Sorry, To', not good, we've stopped the per diems but it isn't doing much good. They're selling their clothes to the dealers now. Lara and I went down to the harbour this morning, just an early morning walk to clear our heads. Looked down and saw Bobby the Diver, the main local connection, in his little fishing boat heading out past the jetty.'

Lara pointed out that Bobby the Diver, the local man for whom there was no waiting, was wearing an Armani jacket. Nathan pointed out that, 'Fuck, he's wearing my Armani jacket.'

'And the wives and girlfriends have arrived now and are lying by the pool. Oh, and we've lost another two hire cars and Bez has broken his shoulder.'

'And lyrics?'

'No lyrics, T, sorry.'

Fuck it.

'I've got to be back in England for some Granada stuff in two days' time, I'll fly home via you, I'll be there tomorrow night. Just hang on Nabs, just hang on.'

If you learn nothing else from this book, you're going to learn where Barbados is. Wilson had assumed that being in the Caribbean, it would be somewhere midway between LAX and LHR. Near Cuba maybe? Fuck that. It's in Venezuela. Honest.

A look at the airline route map was an astonishing recognition of the shaky grasp he had of the Americas. The trip was impossible. The day job inexorable. And he and Yvette flew straight home.

Je ne regrette rien. But he still regrets that.

Not that he'd have made the slightest bit of difference. But he would have liked to have seen the carnage head on. Like the time New Order and Happy Mondays had a party at Peter Gabriel's wonderland studio, Real World, outside Bath.

Ten thousand pounds' worth of damage, and Wilson never made that party either. He just paid for it. And he wasn't paying any more for this party.

But how he would have loved to have been there at midnight on the day they terminated the sessions, how he would have liked to have been with the security guard when his torch lit up first the opened fire doors at the back of the studio complex and then panned left to find Shaun heaving Eddy Grant's two studio sofas into the back of a battered van. On his way into town to swap them for some crack. Would have liked to have been there – wouldn't you?

61
WHAT'S IN A NAME?

Frustration, madness, meltdown. Not all Shaun's fault. His gang members, who had spent five years doing just what their leader said, banging that drum, hitting that guitar just so, were now members of the hit band the Happy Mondays. They were musicians now, famous musicians. They didn't need telling what to do.

Now Shaun was cursed by musicianship and found his refuge in rock and not roll.

Back home, the creative block was uneased. Heavy with confusion, Shaun even took it out on the big mirror in the Dry Bar. Shot it to smithereens. And even that loaded gun didn't set him free.

Back at the hanging table, now leaning a little to the right after Shaun tried to have sex on it during a late night interview with *Select* magazine that got personal, the Factory board wrestled with the unbalanced balance sheet.

'We have to get these albums finished. Phil, can you get over to the Hac? Apparently we can scrape a couple of grand together. If you leave now you can get on down south and intercept the equipment rental guy on the M4. He says he's repossessing the extra outboard stuff we got in at Real World for New Order. Go on, hurry up.'

'And when the two grand's gone, what then?' sang Plato's ghost.

Wilson was serious and still confident of avoiding disaster. They'd survived before.

'We just need someone to pay for the studios and help us out. Get refinanced.'

'By who?'

'Principally, London Records.'

Wilson had spent his recent hectic time in conversations with London Records boss and Polygram executive Roger Ames, who was looking for a bit of Indie.

'London Records,' repeated Wilson.

'Fuck it.' Said Gretton, definitively.

'What's wrong with London Records?'

'The fucking name, for starters.'

'It's just a fucking name, Rob.'

'I fucking hate London.'

'They had to call it something. D'you want me to make a deal with Virgin? How do you feel about virgins?'

'The whole point of doing this thing was that we hated London. That's why we're in Manchester.'

'London town maybe. Not London the record label.'

'You're splitting hairs now, Tony.'

'Splitting hairs, what the fuck do you know about splitting hairs? This is the man who managed two bands both named after fucking Nazis.'

Ooooops, the chairs going backwards again. Gretton gets in a quick knee to the groin. Wilson goes down. Erasmus drags Rob off and sits him back down.

Silence. Maybe thirty seconds.

'You've dropped a bollock, haven't you?'

'Yes, Rob, I've dropped a bollock.'

'A bloody big bollock.'

'Yes, I have, a great big bloody bollock, Rob, a great big one.'

62
FOR WHAT IT'S WORTH

Roger Ames was a suave, handsome music boss, with a wonderful Trinidadian lilt to his accent, that seemed to underline his real love of music and belied his ruthless instincts. 'If you love the music, buy the CD, don't sign the fucking band,' was the most profound advice ever given to an A&R man.

Man went game fishing on holidays back home. And this afternoon he was reeling in his latest catch. He too arrived up through Kelly's stainless-steel tunnel into the spectacular Factory boardroom.

'Great to be here, everybody, great to be here.'

Introductions all round. Even Gretton. He and Ames had met once before, but Rob had difficulty remembering it. That round of negotiations had begun with a Chinese at the Kwok Man, Gretton had done six Sapporos and spent the entire afternoon meeting asleep, flat out on the office sofa.

'Nice table,' said Ames with a small degree of sincerity. 'Alright, I think we have a deal, we've done the numbers and we want to buy you.'

'Buy what?' asked Alan.

'Buy everything. Factory, the lot, buy this table, even the food that's on the table. And a nice spread you've laid out, too.'

'How much?'

'Four million pounds.'

Salvation shouldn't taste so sour. Survival shouldn't come so unwanted.

There was a pause. A long one.

Gretton stared straight ahead. Alan smiled but coldly.

Wilson stood up, bit a lip for a moment, unsure, but finally sure.

'Roger, thank you, we're very grateful for your generous offer and valuing our work at £4 million, very complimentary, but there's a slight problem. You're asking us to sell out and that's a problem. We can't sell out, 'cause we have nothing to sell. You think you're buying our back catalogue, you're buying Joy Division, New Order and the Happy Mondays from us. Well, errrr, you can't buy them from us, 'cause we don't own them.'

'What on earth are you talking about?' from a mystified Ames.

Wilson went to the back wall. They never had gold discs on their walls – these arrogant Mancs were above all that record company shit – but they had framed the napkin inscribed in Wilson's blood. Wilson took it down from its hook and laid it on the red lacquer surface in front of Ames.

'There, you see,' said Wilson, pointing with his finger as Ames tried to decipher 'the contract'.

'"The record company own nothing, the musicians own everything…"'

Ames read on: '"the musicians have the freedom…"'

He looks a bit lost.

Wilson helps out, pointing to the next line: '"… to fuck off. The freedom to fuck off."'

'Ah, yes,' said Ames gratefully. 'You do realize that this means I don't have to talk to you at all?'

'I know.'

'You're completely fucked.'

'Yes, completely fucked. Brilliantly fucked. We wrote this as an insurance. We wrote this so on the day we finally wanted to sell out we wouldn't be able to, see. How can you sell out when you've nothing to sell?'

Some shock, some silence. Some desultory conversation.

The meeting broke up.

Everything was broken up, now.

Call the cops? No, call in the receivers.

63
RUINED IN A DAY

Gretton wasn't going to let the club go down in the midst of all this Factory crap. It wasn't Fac 51, it was the Haçienda. And he would save it. Again an investor was sought, but one much nearer to home. Paul Cons had a financial partner now, had a bit of money. Let's face it, Rob had already borrowed money for the club from his own doormen, so this was clean and dandy. Paul's mate was an accountant.

But when you get new partners, the new partners have questions. About the future of their investment.

And when you get a new set of licensing magistrates, they get an introductory tour.

Honest.

A dozen or so well-appointed magistrates who are responsible for licensing the biggest drug dealers in town, the folks who sell alcohol.

They do the round of the town in a little ten-seat minibus. To get the feel. Which they bloody need, as the Manchester magistrate class still live in Knutsford and wouldn't know a rave from a gymkhana.

And where did their rounds take them around midnight? To the legendary Haçienda. They were greeted just inside the doors with their italic 5 and 1 cut-outs, with a scene resembling an impromptu first-aid station during the Blitz. Walking wounded, bandages and blood.

Seems that at around half-ten a bunch of likely lads from St Helens, a town down the road, midway between Liverpool and Manchester, the very perineum of the North-West – 'taint one thing, 'taint the other – had rambled into the club, headed under the post-modernist arch and turned straight left and headed into Acid Corner, mob-handed. Problem was, this was now Salford Corner, as we briefly mentioned earlier, and the incursion merited horrible reprisals.

It went off.

Badly.

To their credit, the doormen dealt with it quickly and even-handedly and ejected the young Salford who had battered the young St Helens.

Staff first-aided the worst hurt and advised them to stay inside the club to avoid more trouble when they hit the street.

And this was the scene as the magistrates arrived.

Well, it was a bit of excitement for them, wasn't it?

After taking it all in and complaining about one broken bottle on the floor or something equally anal, they moved out onto Whitworth Street and crossed the road to their parked-up minibus.

Good timing. Thirty seconds later, the mob from St Helens left too. Hardly had they got out onto the pavement than two cars screeched up from the direction of Salford, emergency-stopped right outside the club, disgorged half a dozen and all hell broke loose again.

The sound of police sirens and police whistles merged into the pandemonium. And the magistrates were standing beside their minibus, directly across the road. Well, we began with dropped jaws, let's end that way too. Their jaws dropped. They stared on.

A phalanx of policemen with dogs advanced slowly and with menace down Whitworth Street, two of Salford jumped in one of the cars and gunned off in the direction of the Ritz. It was over, thank God.

Passing the venue, the car did a handbrake turn, and screamed back in the direction of the Haçienda. Straight at the melee. One St Helens lad – and don't worry, he survived – had been thrown out into the road.

Salford car took aim, ploughed in and bounced the poor fucker off its windscreen.

This isn't a movie, but it would be nice to have some great Peckinpah slow-mo to capture the trajectory of the blood splats as they spat out across the street and flecked the grey Burberrys of the onlooking magistrates.

Never noticed it before, but a reader looking for resonances will have noticed the blood thing. Two crimson signatures. That spelt the end.

That spelt another closure order from Great Great Greater Manchester Police. One that even George Carman couldn't save them from.

No future.

No investment.

64
LOVE WILL TEAR US APART – THE REMIX

Wilson got a phone call from Don Tonay, back after several years on a beach in the West Indies.

'Come round to the old place.'

The Russel Club was still there. Little changed. Don too. Still a mighty and imposing figure.

'I'm in security now, Tony. Repossession. It's where the money is.'

Two Moss Side dudes shuffled on stage behind Tonay and Tony.

'Alright boys,' says the Don.

And they start up singing to a backing tape.

'Listen to this.'

We are listening to a bad soft-shoe shuffle version of nothing other than 'Love Will Tear Us Apart'.

'Yeah,' says Don, 'it's an old Joy Division song with a soul slant.'

Wilson is weary. So weary he is now even weary of irony. And to be weary of irony is to be as weary as God on the seventh day.

'I know what it is, Don.' And tries to ignore the lift music. And anyway, he's guessed what's coming. His body language at the bar next to Don tells you that. Just a bit slumped. Head down, and that's not to minimize the double chin. It's what fate does to you.

'I've got a repossession early next Sunday morning. Massive job.'

Wilson, blankly, 'Whitworth Street?'

Don is silent.

'The Haçienda?'

'I'm saying fuck all.'

He had said enough.

Wilson turns towards the stage. 'Er, I think I've heard enough lads. I'll call you.'

They shoot horses, apparently.

He turns to Don.

'Thanks.'

65
YOU'LL FIND THE COMPUTERS AND BOOZE IN THE UPSTAIRS OFFICE

There was a last night. The dream recreated for all for one last time. A great fucking night too. The drugs worked one more time, Pickering played, and the people danced, even Ian Curtis danced.

And there were greetings and hugs and comradeship and nostalgia and delirium and inheritance.

'Don't tell me dad, but I'm fucking well out of it.'

Great fucking night.

And Wilson stood at the front of the DJ box, at the end of this revel, with his utterly beautiful partner by his side. She stayed through the bad times too, proving the surmise of that first meeting to be correct.

'Hey!'

Wilson picked up the microphone, the mike the DJs never used, 'cause even though Manchester had invented DJ'ing in the good old days – Jimmy Saville, the first man with twin decks, honest – times had moved on and DJs didn't fucking talk in the modern world.

But it was time to say goodbye. Time to use the microphone.

He uttered some crazy valediction, asking the crowd to please loot the building before leaving. And saying something crap about flowers blooming.

Nice words. But Manchester was blooming anyway. Didn't need the seed bed anymore. Goodbye. Goodbye. Gotta go now. Gotta go now.

66
UP ON THE ROOF

Dawn broke over the Manchester rooftops – cold, early light bringing the tall cranes into relief. Everywhere, the cranes that were building new loft apartment blocks as fast as a kid with his Christmas morning Lego.

Wilson wrapped his long black Yohji overcoat around himself and emerged onto the Haçienda roof to meditate a moment with a good view of his town, an overview as it were.

And there on the roof, he found three of his partners. Three of his colleagues. Three of his lovers, or at least beloved by him. Sitting on the side of the parapet in the lea of the low wall, huddled up against the end of the night chill. They were passing a big spliff.

Wilson walked over. Quietly.

'Listen, T, I'm sorry about everything what's happened man, really sorry.'

'That's alright Shaun, really, fine.'

Maybe he could have given Shaun his favourite quote ever, that 'inexorable modality of life' phrase that Jimmy Joyce slots into *Ulysses* that forces you to go for the dictionary.

But the energy for literary dialogue had at last, equally inexorably, deserted him.

He took the spliff from Rob and took a deep inhale.

His head cocked and his eyes closed a little.

'Bloody good stuff this, where d'you get it?'

'Shaun brought it back from Barbados,' said Alan.

Wilson took another drag. Happy now and at peace.

'There you are, you see, Shaun, it wasn't all a waste of time, was it?'

Not a fucking minute of it.

He passed the joint to Razzer and wandered over to the far end of the roof, and looked at his city.

piecetocam

If I have one downfall, it is an excess of civic pride, a relish for the history and the future of this town, its resourcefulness, its great merchant buildings, its cheap, abundant drugs.

And whilst so thinking, something very strange happened.

There was a whooshing sound, a blur of light, a star shooting from the East from the direction of the Pennine moors. It came into focus and Wilson saw God hovering over his city.

God looked like Wilson in a shabby flowing white dress and with a hair-piece that closely resembled Dumbledore's wig from that Harry Potter movie.

And God said to Wilson:

'Tony, you did a good job. And basically you were right. Shaun is the greatest poet since W.B. Yeats; Joy Division were the greatest band of all time; you probably should have signed The Smiths, but you were right about Mick Hucknall. His music's rubbish and he's a ginger.'

'This is amazing, God. Can I have it in writing?'

'It's already written in the sinews of history and the hearts of men. Vini Reilly, by the way, is due a revival. You might think about a Greatest Hits.'

'That's a very good idea, God.'

'It's good music to chill out to,' said God, understandably imperiously.

'You're right, God.'

'I usually am.'

Whooooooosh. And he's gone.

Wilson walks back over to his mates. Alan has just passed the joint to Shaun. Rob in the middle, bent over against the cold, makes room for Wilson to sit down.

'I just talked to God.'

They pass the joint.

'What did he look like?' asks Alan.

'He looked like me. But with a big white beard, of course. But he looked like me.'

'What do you mean, he looked like you?' Gretton found it a bit early in the day for his mate's bullshit.

'He looked like me. You know what they say in the Bible, God made man in his own image.'

But Gretton had been to a Catholic grammar school too and it wasn't so early he was going to give Wilson any space. It was what these two did. So he came back again, having taken a few seconds to retrieve the joint from Alan.

'Yes, but not a specific man.'

'I know, but I suppose if you had a vision of God, he'd look like you. But you didn't. I did. And he looked like me.'

Should they argue some more? Naw, it's a nice morning. The sun's coming up.

Gretton took another hit on the joint.

'Fucking great gear.'